5T0

ACPL I1 ☑ **YO-BVQ-476**

Y ☐
BEF **DISCARDED**
VIO

DO NOT REMOVE
CARDS FROM POCKET

ALLEN COUNTY PUBLIC LIBRARY

FORT WAYNE, INDIANA 46802

You may return this book to any agency, branch,
or bookmobile of the Allen County Public Library

DEMCO

VIOLENCE AND DRUGS

GILDA BERGER

VIOLENCE

AND DRUGS

Franklin Watts ■ *New York* ■ *London* ■ *Toronto* ■ *Sydney* ■ *1989*

Allen County Public Library
Ft. Wayne, Indiana

Library of Congress Cataloging-in-Publication Data

Berger, Gilda.
Violence and drugs / by Gilda Berger.
p. cm.
Bibliography: p.
Includes index.
Summary: Discusses the correlation between drugs and violent
crime, examining such aspects as drug taking and violence, drug
dealing and violence, and law enforcement and violence.
ISBN 0-531-10818-x
1. Narcotics and crime—United States—Juvenile literature.
2. Violent crimes—United States—Juvenile literature. [1. Drug
abuse and crime.] I. Title.
HV5825.B49 1989
364.2—dc20 89-34154 CIP AC

Copyright © 1989 by Gilda Berger
All rights reserved
Printed in the United States of America
5 4 3 2 1

CONTENTS

Chapter One
*The Drugs-Violence
Connection*
■ 9 ■

Chapter Two
*Drug Taking and
Violence*
■ 19 ■

Chapter Three
*Low-Level
Drug Dealing
and Violence*
■ 33 ■

Chapter Four
*Middle-Level
Drug Dealing
and Violence*
■ 46 ■

Chapter Five
*Top-Level
Drug Trafficking
and Violence*
■ *60* ■

Chapter Six
*Law Enforcement
and Violence*
■ *75* ■

Chapter Seven
*Policy Making
and Violence*
■ *87* ■

Source Notes 99

Bibliography 106

Index 109

VIOLENCE AND DRUGS

CHAPTER

1

THE DRUGS-VIOLENCE CONNECTION

■ *A forty-seven year-old woman lives in a drug-infested neighborhood. One night, during a gunfight between rival dealers, a stray bullet smashes through her kitchen window and kills her on the spot.*

■ *Terrified bus passengers dive beneath their seats as police charge on board and arrest a man who has commandeered the bus at gunpoint. The man later admits to being high on crack at the time of the incident.*

■ *The body of a young man, a drug-gang member dead of gunshot wounds, lies in a coffin inside the quiet church. During the service, bullets suddenly shatter the peace as rival drug-gang members shoot at the mourners with automatic weapons.*

■ *Drug dealers in Colombia gun down the security chief of an overseas airline because he reported finding a 440-pound (198-kg) shipment of cocaine hidden in the tires of a 747 jetliner bound for Miami.*

■ *A notorious drug lord is stabbed to death in Leavenworth Penitentiary, Kansas, while serving a life sentence for drug trafficking.*

Is violence flooding the land? Have robberies, assaults, killings of police, and gang-member assassinations become more commonplace? Is the use, sale, and trafficking of illegal drugs responsible for the growing number of murders and other serious crimes across America?

DRUG USE AND CRIME

According to James Stewart, director of the federal government's National Institute of Justice (NIJ), people who use one of the major illegal drugs—heroin, cocaine, PCP, LSD, etc.—commit four to six times as many crimes as non–drug users. Or, put another way, half of all persons arrested for crime are drug users.[1] Further, in three-quarters of all child-abuse cases, one or both parents are addicted to drugs.[2] Addicts in America, it is said, are responsible for as many as 50 million crimes each year.[3] As New York City police commissioner Benjamin Ward declared: "I believe the crime problem in America today is the drug problem."[4]

The leading causes of death among teenagers and young addicts—unintentional injuries, suicide, and homicide—are in many cases linked to drug abuse.[5] Major cities, including San Diego, New Orleans, Los Angeles, Philadelphia, Miami, and Detroit, report drug-related homicides in the 15 to 30 percent range.[6] New York City in 1988 had a record percentage of killings linked directly to drugs: over 42 percent of all the city's slayings were drug-related, compared to 38 percent in 1987 and 35 percent in 1986.[7]

Many law enforcement officers consider a personal history of drug abuse to be an important predictor of serious criminal activity. These experts study the many connections between drugs and crime. They consider everything from the way drug abuse and trafficking affects users, to the impact of drug-related crime on our society.

One very recent and important study that showed clear links between the problems of crime and drugs was the

Justice Department's 1986 *Survey of Inmates of State Correctional Facilities.* The study found high levels of drug use prior to the commission of the crimes for which the prisoners were serving time. Two-thirds of state prison inmates said they had been using illegal drugs on a daily or near daily basis in the month before their current offense. Nineteen percent said they were using so-called major drugs—heroin, methadone, cocaine, PCP, or LSD—regularly. More than half of the inmates said they had used a major drug sometime in the past; 36 percent had done drugs on a regular basis. Among all inmates, 25 percent reported using a major drug in the month before the current offense.[8]

Although regular drug abusers were a minority of the inmate population, experts believe this group may be responsible for a disproportionate share of crimes. Research with addicts has shown that they commit crimes more frequently than do nonaddicts. Moreover, data from the inmate survey showed a relationship between the degree of illegal drug use and the number of prior convictions: the greater the use of the major illegal drugs, the more convictions the inmate was likely to report. Those who had used a major illegal drug regularly in the past or in the month before the offense usually had three or more prior convictions.

The connection between illegal drug use and criminal activity is especially strong among young offenders. Nearly half of the juveniles in correctional institutions in 1987 for violent crimes were under the influence of drugs or alcohol when they committed their offenses. Nearly 60 percent had used drugs regularly, once a week or more, for at least a month. "Many of the juvenile offenders had criminal histories that were just as extensive as those of adults in state prisons," said Steven R. Schlesinger, director of the Bureau of Justice Statistics.[9]

Despite the many linkages that have been found between drugs and crime, however, the exact relationship between them is still not clear. Although drugs and crime are often found together, many other factors may contribute to the start or continuation of criminal behavior. Those who are inclined to be criminals may express that criminality through drug use as well as in other ways. Crime existed long before the nation's drug epidemic came into being, some argue.

During the 1970s, Paul J. Goldstein of Narcotic and Drug Research, Inc., outlined three possible ways to look at the drug-crime connection. These ways, or models, have had a great influence on research over the last twenty years. One model considered addiction and the effect of short-term or long-term use of specific substances on the individual's personality. The second model looked at drug users' need for money to finance their habit. The third and last way considered violent crime as an integral part of illegal drug trafficking and distribution.[10]

The major types of violent crime may be defined this way:

Arson. The willful and malicious burning of someone else's property, or of your own property to collect insurance.

Assault. An unlawful physical attack, or an attempted or threatened attack, with or without a weapon. An attempted or threatened attack without a weapon, or an attack that results in only minor injury, is called *simple assault.*

Aggravated assault. An attack that results in serious bodily injury, or the threat or attempt with a weapon to inflict bodily injury or death.

Battery. Actual physical force or violence applied to another person.

Homicide. The killing of one human being by another.

Rape. Completed or attempted unlawful sexual intercourse through the use of force or the threat of force.

Robbery. The forcible taking of goods or money directly from a person by force or threat of force, with or without a weapon.[11]

Efforts to stop violent crime through the prevention and control of drug abuse center on establishing a cause and effect between crime and drugs. Does drug abuse lead to criminal behavior? Why do criminals commit more crimes when they are using drugs? Are most crimes committed to get money to purchase illegal drugs? How does the heavy use of illegal drugs lead the user into a subculture of crime and violence?

VIOLENT CRIMES UNDER
THE INFLUENCE OF DRUGS

Although it is widely accepted that drug abuse fuels crime, a cause-and-effect relationship is very hard to establish. Many homicides, for example, are considered drug-related because of the presence of drugs in the bloodstream of the victim or killer, drugs or drug paraphernalia found at the scene of the crime, or the victim's or murderer's known drug connections. It is this kind of evidence that often establishes the drug-crime connection.

There are some experts who do not believe that criminals commit more crime when they are on drugs. They hold this view despite the fact that a significant proportion of those convicted of violent crimes were under the influence of drugs at the time of the offense. These figures run as high as 28.6 percent of those convicted of assault and 32 percent of those convicted of rape.[12] The reason they give is that at the time of arrest, it is difficult to determine whether the person had been acting under the influence of a drug while committing the offense. Often, though, the crime springs from a need to get money for drugs or a general involvement in the drug culture.

Certain drugs, such as crack, amphetamines, and PCP, are known to cause excitability and irrationality. The result of this can be an increased likelihood of performing acts of wanton violence. In the words of one addict: "Many times when you're sick you might do things you don't normally [do]. You can get so desperate and uptight that you don't see straight. . . ."[13]

Crack, for example, is a highly addictive form of cocaine. Many recent studies show that a very high fraction of those arrested used crack. But even here, some researchers hold that this does not mean that this form of cocaine causes crime. According to Mark Kleiman, a Harvard University researcher, the results show only "that among poor, urban young men cocaine penetration is far higher than anyone would have guessed."[14]

VIOLENT CRIMES TO SUPPORT A DRUG HABIT

Illegal drugs are very expensive, and regular drug use makes it very hard for the addict to earn an income legally. To finance their costly habit, many users commit crimes and engage in other kinds of questionable activities to get the money they need to purchase drugs.

The 1986 *Survey of Inmates* showed that users of major illegal drugs, especially daily users, were least likely to have been employed and most likely to have been both unemployed and not seeking work. Further, users of major drugs were far more likely than nonusers to report that they received income from illegal activities during the time they were last free. Nearly half of daily users of a major illegal drug said they had received some part of their income from illegal sources compared to less than 10 percent of those who never used a major illegal drug.[15]

Many researchers have tried to find out which comes first, drug abuse or criminality. Among nearly 80 percent of inmates who reported some illegal drug use at some time in the past, the median age of first use was fifteen years. The first arrest, probation, or incarceration took place, on average, between the ages of sixteen and nineteen. Yet in the majority of cases, the drugs used before the first arrest were usually not one of the major drugs.[16] This finding, that major-drug use comes *after* the beginning of a criminal career, comes out in other research as well. It seems to refute the common assumption that drugs cause crime.

Generally speaking, the onset of crime (even when it preceded drug use) as well as the size of a drug habit seems to be connected to the intensity of criminal activity. A typical daily heroin user consumes about $17,000 worth of drugs a year as compared to only $5,000 for irregular users. And daily heroin users also commit about five times as many robberies and burglaries as irregular users.[17]

VIOLENT CRIME AS PART OF THE DRUG CULTURE

Violent crime has always been an integral part of illegal drug trafficking and distribution. Violence associated with disputes over drugs has been common to the drug scene since its inception. A drug dealer beats up an addict who owes him or her money and doesn't pay. A drug distributor sends in armed thugs to take over the drug trade in an entire city. A drug lord burns down the factory of a rival drug producer.

What is more common today than formerly is that many of those selling drugs on the street are juveniles. These juveniles are also committing a disproportionate number of the violent crimes. The problem starts early on. As Shirley Taylor of Washington, D.C., asks: "How can you keep a kid in school if he knows that there's big, fast money to be had out on the street?" She continues, "He [the young would-be drug dealer] looks at his peers, wearing those fat gold chains and the designer running suits and driving those big high-wheel trucks equipped with booming stereos, and he knows he can have it all himself in a matter of weeks or months—if he lives. So he loses interest fast in the classroom or some restaurant job at minimum wage."[18]

Most drug abusers become part of the criminal community as soon as they become heavily involved with illegal substances. And membership in this community may be more responsible for their frequent acts of violence than the effects of the drugs they abuse or even their need for money to buy drugs. Territorial disputes between rival drug dealers, robberies, violent retaliations, elimination of informers, punishment for selling adulterated, phony, or otherwise "bad" drugs, punishment for failing to pay one's debts, and general disputes over drugs or drug paraphernalia—all are common to the drug culture.

DRUG–CRIME TRENDS

The drug problem emerged in the early 1960s when great numbers of people began to experiment with marijuana and LSD. Widespread heroin and cocaine abuse followed in the 1970s, and crack, PCP, amphetamines, barbiturates, and inhalants in the 1980s. By 1985, 37 percent (compared to 2 percent in 1960) of all Americans over the age of twelve—some 70 million people in all—had used an illegal drug at least once. Twelve percent of the population—some 23 million people—are current users, according to a recent national household survey.[19]

Starting in the early 1970s, people began to be alarmed by the high crime rate. According to a 1972 Gallup Poll, about half of those surveyed were afraid to walk in their neighborhoods at night. Most cited drug addiction as one of the main reasons for the high crime rate.[20]

President Richard M. Nixon spoke in January 1973 of drugs as "public enemy number one, destroying the most precious resource we have—our young people—and breeding lawlessness, violence, and death." He said that "crime in the streets" cost the nation roughly $18 billion a year.[21]

Since the 1970s, the public has cried out for tougher laws, and by and large this is what has happened: The population of federal and state prisons swelled from 200,000 in 1970 to 550,000 in 1988. Problems due to prison overcrowding presently exist in every state of the nation. Officials find they cannot afford to continue building prisons at an average cost of $50,000 to $75,000 a cell and are being forced to consider alternatives to incarceration.

Perhaps as a result of the nation's concern over crime and drugs, many efforts have been made to curb drug abuse. Experts tell us that the worst of the drug epidemic now appears to be over. The most recent data conclusions, based on the last National Household survey taken in 1985, indicate a shift away from illegal drug use among Americans. High school seniors, for the first time in more than a decade, show a drop in cocaine use. The use of other drugs, including marijuana, has been declining for several years. With the exception of crack, drug use appears to have leveled off, except for school dropouts and the poor in the inner cities.

The decline, if it continues, may have something to do with certain changes in society's attitudes toward illicit drug use. Dr. David F. Musto, a Yale psychiatrist, believes Americans may be reaching the end of their thirty-year love affair with illegal drugs. People no longer feel that there is a positive side to the use of illegal drugs— that they can be innocent or even occasionally helpful. "By the mid-1980s," Dr. Musto said, "a consensus had been established in American society that any drug use was a dangerous sign—and a consensus that an individual was not an atom but was part of society."[22]

Despite present high levels of crime, the drop in drug use between 1981 and 1986 was accompanied by a decline in the nation's crime level. The exception was 1987, however, when the number of personal crimes—a category that includes rape, robbery, assault, and murder—rose by nearly 250,000, or 1.8 percent, to more than 19 million.[23]

Experts analyzing the data suggest that the size of the most crime-prone age group, those in their mid-to late teens, has shrunk in the 1980s. They say this trend will continue until the early 1990s, when it is expected that crime levels will turn upward once again.

The slight crime increase in 1987 was thought to indicate a greater concentration of low-income individuals in the age group where most crime occurs—during youth. Juvenile crimes of violence are on the increase. Shootings by teenagers are driving homicide rates up. And the overall crime rates in 1987 matched the all-time record highs of the mid-1970s. In New York City, Detroit, Los Angeles, and Chicago, drug-related crimes proliferated with the spread of cocaine and its derivative, crack.

Washington, Atlanta, Miami, Boston, Philadelphia, St. Louis, Baltimore, Dallas, and New York, too, all reported steeply rising crime rates, with teens responsible for a growing number of killings, many of them over drugs. Despite a crackdown on drugs in Washington, the crime rate, driven by the demand for drugs, was up 15 percent in 1988. This is five times the increase recorded by most other large American cities. In some parts of Washington, the rate is up a staggering 40 percent![24]

CONCLUSION

Opinions differ sharply on the degree of devastation caused by the drug epidemic. To Lois Haight Herrington, chairperson of the White House Congress for a Drug-Free America, drug abuse will determine "whether we pass into history as yet another once-proud civilization eaten away from within." But to Arnold S. Trebach, a political science professor at American University in Washington, D.C., drug abuse is not destroying the nation. "Most people who use most drugs are not in trouble with them," Trebach says.[25]

In this book we will consider some of the current knowledge on how drug abuse affects crime. We will look at drug-crime linkages on every level of drug use and drug trafficking.

CHAPTER

2

DRUG TAKING AND VIOLENCE

■ *The body of a fourteen-year-old girl was found on a rubble-strewn railroad embankment used by crack addicts. The girl had been sexually assaulted and bludgeoned to death. She had passed the embankment on a shortcut to the store to buy a newspaper.*

■ *A mother of four children and her friend were killed when an auto driven by a teenager ran a stop sign and slammed into their car. The police said the young man had been drinking.*

■ *A fire in a two-story wood-frame building described as a crack den claimed the lives of two people and sent five others, including three fire fighters, to the hospital. The remains of a gas mixture apparently used as a heat source for crack production were found in the ground-floor apartment.*

■ *A seventeen-year-old student was raped inside a college dormitory by two men who were guests at a party on campus. According to police, the men were intoxicated at the time.*

■ *A man, in a fit of crack-induced madness, cut off his own hand.*

The use of illegal or legal mind-altering substances—whether they be alcohol, heroin, cocaine, LSD, PCP, or whatever—has long been associated with crime and violent behavior. The violence may lead the person under the influence of a drug to harm himself or herself in a drug-related accident or suicide. Or, drug consumption may, in some individuals and some settings, unleash violent behaviors—rape, homicide, assault, robbery, mugging, or reckless actions—that harm their victims.

Although violence is rarely attributed *only* to the influence of drugs, there certainly is an association between drug use and criminality. Many drugs of abuse are powerful chemicals that can and do affect behavior. The specific effects depend on how they are used, by whom, in what settings, and in what amounts.

ALCOHOL AND
VIOLENT CRIME

Alcohol is thought to be involved in some 10,000 murders annually in the United States, and to lead to a similar number of suicides. Heavy drinking is also believed to lower inhibitions and affect judgment. These effects increase the likelihood of violent behavior such as acts of robbery, burglary, and mugging.

Many rape victims report that their assailants had been drinking before the attack. Alcohol also plays a role in half the nation's 44,000 highway deaths every year. And alcohol abuse may contribute to patterns of delinquent behavior in young people by reducing inhibitions and encouraging misbehavior.[1]

Alcohol is most often implicated in male criminality. Different studies link youthful alcohol use to juvenile offenses and to crimes of vengeance and passion. One California study found that drinking delinquents committed significantly more crimes of assault than nondrinkers.[2]

One example taken from a recent newspaper account tells of a seventeen-year-old man accused of attempted murder, assault, criminal possession of a weapon, and resisting arrest in connection with an attack on his former girlfriend. According to the woman, the accused was in an alcohol-induced rage when he attacked her. As the attorney said, the young man "drank beer and other liquor until he reached the state that he was no longer able to act as a thinking rational person."[3]

Alcohol can destroy lives in another way. Because it affects specific skills required to drive safely, it is a factor in thousands of automobile accidents every year. To take just one stark example of drunken driving, multiple counts of murder were brought against thirty-four-year-old Larry Mahoney, who drove his pickup truck the wrong way down an interstate highway in Kentucky and slammed head on into a bus. In the crash and fire that followed, twenty-seven people were killed, most of them teenagers. The police said Mahoney's blood-alcohol level was 0.24, three times the level designated as "impaired" and more than twice the level most states set as "drunk."[4]

Experts see a rising public intolerance for drunken driving throughout the country. More than 500 DWI (driving while intoxicated) laws have been passed in this regard. Such measures have had some effect, but progress has been mostly confined to social drinkers. As John Grant, director of the National Commission Against Drunk Driving, said: "An alcoholic . . . doesn't give a damn, especially after drinking."[5]

Murders, suicides, and traffic deaths are not the only violence linked to alcohol abuse. There is now considerable evidence that countless babies of drinking mothers are born ill and deformed each year. "When a pregnant woman drinks, the fetus drinks, too," said Jane Kirkpatrick, assistant professor of nursing at Purdue University. Unfortunately, she added, the baby who is victim has no say in the matter. "But the child will have to live with the effects of alcohol [fetal alcohol syndrome] the rest of his or her life."[6]

HEROIN AND VIOLENCE

Traditionally viewed as one of the "hardest drugs," heroin is a water-soluble powder that is sometimes sniffed but more often injected intravenously. Upon absorption, heroin stimulates and then depresses the activity of the central nervous system. The initial rush, or surge of pleasure, is followed by a feeling of detachment or a dreamlike state that lasts from two to six hours. Heroin's addictive quality depends on the quantity, frequency, and duration of use. Strong addiction causes marked physical (flulike) symptoms on withdrawal.

Heroin addiction peaked in the early 1970s, then tapered off. The U.S. Drug Enforcement Administration (DEA) estimates that there are presently about 500,000 heroin addicts and users in the United States.[7] The DEA believes that many thousands more use heroin occasionally. The average age of heroin abusers has been rising progressively, suggesting that they are mostly long-term addicts.[8]

Even though heroin use has not grown over the past decade, experts worry about the drug's greater purity and new trends in its use. Two new types of heroin or heroin-like drugs, "Black Tar" and "China White," which are up to 99 percent pure, are responsible for a recent rise in overdose deaths. There is new evidence, too, that most heroin addicts tend to use a variety of other drugs in addition to heroin.

Methadone is a common treatment for heroin addiction. Methadone blocks heroin craving while permitting normal functioning. Advocates of methadone therapy claim that this treatment can practically eliminate heroin use and thus reduce the need to commit street crime for monetary gain. Other research shows that methadone appears to work best when there is only minimal drug involvement, delinquent behavior, and emotional disturbance.[9]

Experts who study the heroin problem usually portray the addict as an unemployed, minority, urban-ghetto male with little education who commits crimes to support his habit. A 1985 study of heroin users in the east and central Harlem neighborhoods of New York City found the following: [10]

75 percent were male.
55 percent were black.
44 percent were Hispanic.
36 percent were under thirty years of age.
61 percent had less than eleven years of education.
81 percent were unemployed.

The crime rate for these heroin users was an amazing 1,075 crimes per person per year. Crimes included those against people and property, as well as drug offenses. Once thought to be passive and non-violent, heroin-using offenders recently have been shown to be just as likely as other offenders to commit such crimes as homicide, sexual assault, and arson. They are even more likely to commit robbery and weapons offenses. Many were surprised by these findings, which show heroin addicts to be more violent than was previously believed.

Research also suggests that many of the crimes committed by heroin addicts are unrelated to heroin abuse. Most heroin addicts had committed crimes before they became heroin users. The average age of an addict at the time of his or her first crime is less than fifteen years. Most don't become involved with heroin until nearly age nineteen. However, while heroin use may not start a criminal career, it can often intensify and perpetuate the violent behavior.

Researchers from Baltimore analyzed patterns of crime for 354 "typical" heroin addicts. Over a nine-year period, their crime rates dropped to relatively low levels when they had little or no heroin and became much higher when they were actively addicted. In other words, the level of crime tended to rise and fall with drug usage.

Doctors are beginning to notice a high rate of suicide among heroin and cocaine drug users. Many of these addicts are victims of AIDS, a serious communicable disease that destroys the body's immune system. The addicts contract the disease through the sharing of contaminated needles. One AIDS patient left a note indicating that he gave up and killed himself because his cries for help went unanswered. In other patients, the deaths were blamed on mental derangement caused by the virus's effect on their brains.

The spread of AIDS may also be responsible for a wave of violence among heroin users. This violence revolves around the sale or sharing of needles and syringes, called "works." Not only can heroin users who share the same hypodermic needles with other addicts pass the AIDS virus from one individual to another, but infected individuals can transmit the virus to their sexual partners. And babies born to infected mothers can suffer the ravages of the disease.

Fear of contracting the disease from unclean works quickly develops into fights and killings. The usual victims are addicts who have used another's works without permission and dealers who have duped their customers by selling them used works as new.

COCAINE AND VIOLENCE

Cocaine use is currently the major national drug concern. The number of regular users is up to an astounding 5.8 million (in 1985); the number of people who occasionally use cocaine is about 12 million.[11]

Cocaine, for the most part, is used in one of two forms. Cocaine hydrochloride, a white crystalline powder, is usually snorted, or inhaled through the nose, from a thin line of powder. It can also be dissolved in water and injected or prepared in its free-base form and smoked. (The other form of cocaine, called crack, is discussed later.)

Cocaine in all its forms often incites aggressive behavior and paranoia. Initial effects typically include excitation, increased alertness, insomnia, loss of appetite, increased heart rate, increased respiration, and increased blood pressure. These consequences often appear after just one use.

In both the powder and free-base form, today's cocaine is purer and therefore more likely to cause overdose, respiratory failure, and cardiac arrest than before. According to Dr. Mark Gold, director of research at Fair Oaks Hospital in New Jersey: "We have no way of predicting who'll die from the drug and who won't. It could be a regular user or it could be a first-time user."[12]

Approximately 25 million Americans have tried cocaine; of that number, between 5 and 6 million use it at least once per month. Of the regular users, it is estimated that almost half may be considered addicted.[13] Cocaine-related hospital emergencies almost tripled over a four-year period, from about 5,200 in 1982 to about 14,000 in 1986—a rise due in part to the cumulative effects of past drug use.[14]

The use of cocaine in combination with other drugs appears to be increasing. Fifty-nine percent of cocaine-related deaths in 1984 involved other drugs particularly alcohol, heroin, or PCP. Some addicts combine cocaine and heroin and inject the mixture, which is called a "speedball." They claim that the cocaine in the speedball gives them an immediate pleasurable rush, which is then followed by a long period of euphoria from the heroin. The heroin also works to offset the depression that often comes after cocaine use.

An autopsy report showed that American Ballet Theater star Patrick Bissell died of an overdose of a combination of cocaine, methadone, and other drugs. Similarly, actor John Belushi's final, drug-filled days in Hollywood were spent in a frenzied drive for both cocaine and heroin. His life ended after a five-day binge in which he was injected with a series of speedballs.[15]

Cocaine use is believed to have played a part in causing the crash of an American Airlines plane on January 19, 1988. Officials detected traces of cocaine in the body of the pilot, who was among the nine people killed in the crash. Dr. Gold said detection of even a small amount of cocaine was evidence of recent use and intoxication. "The question is, did that cause any judgment problems?"[16]

In a highly publicized trial of late 1988 and early 1989, it was found that Joel B. Steinberg was using cocaine heavily on the night he battered his six-year-old daughter, Lisa, inflicting the injuries that led to her death three days later. Law-enforcement officers said that Steinberg was a very heavy drug user.[17]

Cities where cocaine use has become widespread, are experiencing an increasing number of cases of violent, erratic, and paranoid behavior among heavy users. Doctors recognize this as a special, drug-induced condition, which they call "cocaine psychosis." In one recent instance a man, apparently suffering from cocaine psychosis, held four people hostage for thirty hours in a New York City apartment.[18]

CRACK AND VIOLENCE

The type of cocaine that the police are currently most concerned about is crack. Crack is a smokable form of cocaine that is sold in small, cheap units. The low cost makes crack accessible to vast numbers of people who could not afford to buy the much more expensive cocaine powder for inhaling.

Crack has largely replaced heroin as the drug of choice in the inner city. And police officials are seeing rising numbers of homicides and violent, unpredictable behavior among crack abusers.

"In all my years of experience," said Commissioner Harold E. Adams of the Nassau County (New York State) Department of Drug and Alcohol Addiction, "I've never seen a drug that's more frightening and more of a menace than crack because of the violent reaction and nature of those addicted to the substance." Dr. Donald Ian MacDonald, formerly of the U.S. Alcohol, Drug Abuse and Mental Health Administration, adds that crack is one of the most powerfully addictive substances known.[19]

Because crack delivers ten times the impact of cocaine powder that is snorted, casual use can cause death from heart or respiratory failure. Crack smokers also run an increased risk of addiction and paranoid psychosis.

Many people who are mentally ill or emotionally disturbed can be made much worse by such drugs as cocaine and crack. These drugs have pushed patients who are marginally ill into full-blown psychoses, including agitated, violent behavior. In the same way, the drugs have worsened the condition of those who were improving. The drug "unravels treatment," according to Jeffrey Gunberg, director of a shelter psychiatry program.[20]

As an example of crack-induced behavior, a crack-smoking man led police on a 10-mile (16-km) car chase at speeds up to 70 miles (116 km) per hour. The chase finally ended when the car he was driving collided with that of a motorist, who was killed immediately. The two autos then careened onto the sidewalk, injuring a thirteen-year old schoolgirl and a crossing guard who was standing next to her.

Wayne County (Michigan) prosecutor John O'Hair estimates that 70 percent of all local crimes are drug-related and much of the havoc is crack-fueled. "Crack is a pick-me-up, a big rush. So there is a tendency to become more active, more aggressive, and more violent."[21]

Research shows that crack and cocaine users are among the most active of all criminal offenders and are most likely to commit robbery, assault, and property crimes. Over 90 percent of those arrested for robbery in New York City's borough of Manhattan in late 1986 were found to be drug-positive, mainly for cocaine.[22]

High on any list of tragic results due to crack use are the number of babies born to addicted mothers. Such newborns tend to be lethargic and irritable. Many suffer a range of health defects that often lead to an early death.

Because a crack high is very intense but extremely short-lived, cravings occur at greater frequency, and users require a never-ending supply of money and drugs. This explains the close association between crack and violence. The users, in order to meet their need for more and more drugs, turn to crime—and often violent crime—against victims in and outside of their families.

MARIJUANA
AND VIOLENCE

The unique psychoactive drug marijuana, or pot, is made from the dried leaves and flowers of the cannabis plant. Marijuana is widely cultivated and used. It can be smoked in a pipe or as a cigarette, or it can be ingested in food or drink. Hashish, which is also extracted from the cannabis plant, contains a higher concentration of tetrahydrocannabinol (THC), marijuana's psychoactive ingredient. In cake form, hashish is usually smoked in a pipe. Hashish oil can also be mixed with tobacco and smoked that way.

The effects of marijuana use have been the subject of misunderstanding for decades. In 1936, for example, the film *Reefer Madness* portrayed marijuana as causing instant violence and insanity. In 1972, the National Commission on Marijuana and Drug Abuse took the opposite view: "No conclusive evidence exists of any physical damage, disturbances of bodily processes or proven human fatalities attributable solely to even high doses of marijuana."[23]

Today it is known that marijuana can produce varying degrees of intoxication. Some authorities say marijuana and hashish are nonaddictive, while others claim they produce a psychological dependency.

Marijuana is commonly considered "the most chemically complex of all commonly used illegal drugs." It contains 421 known chemicals that, when smoked, are combined into more than 2,000 different chemical compounds.

The drug is variously classified as a stimulant, depressant, and hallucinogen because of the many different effects it has on the users.

THC, the active ingredient in marijuana, is fat-soluble and remains in the body for a long time. Short- and long-term effects of marijuana abuse include difficulties with memory, learning, and perception. Heavy users frequently experience wild mood swings; fear and anxiety often follow sensations of relaxation and abandon. Some individuals may suffer bizarre hallucinations or harbor thoughts of suicide. New supplies of U.S.-grown marijuana seem to be producing more-toxic effects in users.

Although there is no clear evidence that marijuana leads to crime or that users are associated with criminal groups, the substance has been implicated in accidents that occurred as a result of users' poor perception or errors in judgment.

One notorious example is the 1988 train crash near Chase, Maryland, in which sixteen people died and 175 were injured. According to the National Transportation Board, the accident was probably caused by the impaired performance of a Conrail engineer high on marijuana and alcohol. The engineer passed two stop signals and then slammed into an oncoming Amtrak train traveling 125 miles an hour. One Conrail crewman later told Congress that the railroad industry is riddled with workers who use marijuana and other drugs on the job and drink large amounts of beer. He estimated that between 10 and 50 percent of the railroad workers use drugs.[24]

Scientists now agree that marijuana can cause a number of health effects. The distortion of perception, the reduced ability to think clearly and use good judgment, and the lower level of motor skills impact greatly on users' ability to drive safely. Marijuana has been held responsible for many times the number of accidents caused by drivers who have not used the drug.

DESIGNER DRUGS
AND VIOLENCE

Many illicit drugs, such as heroin, cocaine, and marijuana, are derived from plants. Some drugs, though, do not occur in nature. They are the synthetic drugs, produced from chemicals. These synthetic drugs are sometimes called "designer drugs." Since they have chemical structures similar to those of natural drugs, they produce similar effects.

The use of synthetic drugs is widespread in the United States. Although most of these drugs are used for medical purposes, some are abused by individuals from all socioeconomic groups. It is estimated that more than 6 million Americans used synthetic drugs for nonmedical purposes in 1982.[25]

Hallucinogens make up one group of synthetic drugs. They can alter the user's mood and in large doses cause delusions and hallucinations. The resulting impaired judgment may lead the user to harm himself or herself or inflict harm on others.

The two most important synthetic hallucinogens are known by their initials, LSD or PCP. LSD, or lysergic acid diethylamide, was originally synthesized in 1938 and used for a short time to help treat psychoses, including schizophrenia. As a drug of abuse, it is ingested. PCP, or phencyclidine, is a liquid that is put on tobacco, marijuana, or other plant material and then smoked. It was first synthesized as a veterinary anesthetic in the 1950s.

LSD is less widely used today than it was in the 1960s, when it was a favorite in the "hippie" movement. PCP, also called angel dust, is popular among lower- and middle-class users in big cities such as Los Angeles and Washington. However, it is virtually unknown in many parts of the country.

The effects of LSD range from dizziness and perceptions of bright lights and kaleidoscopic images to convulsions. PCP can cause convulsions, heart and lung failures, and psychotic disorders. Stored in the body's fatty tissues, PCP can be released into the blood stream long after it is ingested. It is notorious for causing bizarre and violent behavior, driving some users to commit assault, rape, or murder. Feelings of omnipotence sometimes lead a PCP user to suicidal behavior, such as walking in front of a speeding car or jumping out of a window.

Some heroin addicts are now taking a synthetic drug called China White that is a slightly altered form of Fentanyl, a widely used surgical anesthetic. It produces the same reactions in the user as heroin, but is over a hundred times more powerful.

A psychedelic drug nicknamed Ecstasy is also currently in vogue. Ecstasy is a combination of a synthetic mescaline and an amphetamine. Pharmacologists and law-enforcement agencies warn that Ecstasy is psychologically addictive and can cause long-term damage. Although users say they enjoy the hours of euphoria it produces, some admit to accidents or bouts of uncontrollable paranoia months after taking it. One unfortunate victim tried to climb a live electrical wire. And a twenty-two-year-old fashion model told how she got the same mental flashes of death and destruction while off Ecstasy that she had while on the drug.

Certain synthetic drugs have a close association with crime. A study of all arrestees in Washington, D.C., from May 1984 to April 1985 found the hallucinogen PCP to be the drug most often detected in those arrested. An average of over 30 percent of all adults arrested in Washington during this period tested positive for PCP use. A similar study of almost 5,000 males arrested in New York City in 1984 found that 12 percent of those arrested had PCP in their bodies.[26]

Richard Kirkwood, on trial for the fatal torching of an eighteen-room house, where twelve people were sleeping, was charged with ten counts of second-degree murder and two counts of arson. The thirty-year-old man apparently had been drinking heavily and smoking marijuana and PCP when he set the house afire. He was still high that day and the next when he told friends and police that he'd started the blaze.[27]

CONCLUSION

Drugs are not "criminogenic" in the sense that they force users to commit crime. Yet the evidence is clear that drug abuse is related to crime. The crime is of two kinds: crime to support the habit and those associated with drug dealing. Also, violent behavior is directly related to the actual effects of the drugs.

The immediate results of drugs in the user may vary from pleasant sensations to violent mood changes, from distorted perception to a loss of motor control. These, in turn, can lead to further changes, such as an impaired ability to drive and violent aggression. Consequences can be as simple as a fender bender or as serious as the loss of life.

Statistics show that drug-related violence is rarely attributable only to the influence of drugs. Those who use drugs themselves usually deal in them. Often, they must engage in violent crime to support their costly habit or to profit from the buying and selling of drugs—the subject of the next chapter.

CHAPTER

3

LOW-LEVEL DRUG DEALING AND VIOLENCE

■ *Robert is a seller of crack. He sells the drug "24-7"—dealer talk for twenty-four hours a day, seven days a week. Buyers sit and smoke crack in his apartment until their money runs out. People who are fleeing the police hide out in his apartment. And drug dealers who have been shot or stabbed on the street use his apartment as an emergency room.*

■ *Sixteen-year-old Calvin began using drugs when he was ten. Today he supports his drug habit working for a dealer who pays him $100 for an eight-hour shift. He carries an automatic pistol and says he used it once to settle an account with a loan shark who demanded Calvin pay back a $40 loan with $100 a week later.*

■ *Six-foot, four-inch James drives a big, fancy white Lincoln Town Car and wears expensive clothes. He acts like he owns the projects he roams. Although he doesn't sell drugs, he makes lots of money from the drug trade. People give him money if they want to sell drugs in his territory. "Five thousand here and ten thousand there," he says. "Some people say it is extortion, but I don't ask for it. They just give it to me."*

Low-level dealers perform a variety of roles in the drug trade. Generally speaking, they assist large-scale sellers and distributors. They run errands, act as lookouts, and make deliveries of money or drugs. They are the front-line soldiers in the battles for territory and to collect debts. These dealers also do some street-level selling. Such individuals are likely to play more than one role during a typical day and have a career that lasts several years until death, prison, or serious injury brings it to an end.

PREPARING FOR
THE DRUG TRADE

In rapidly growing numbers, unskilled, poorly educated people in inner-city areas are finding drug dealing the most lucrative career option available to them. Many children enticed into the drug culture at an early age drop out of school and by their mid-teens enter the violent world of drug dealing and distribution.

In his book *The Dream Sellers*, Richard H. Blum describes drug dealing among the youth of the black urban ghettos of Oakland, California, and the surrounding Bay area. According to Blum, some children show a propensity for drugs and violence as early as age six. Even at this early age, they get a reputation for being "bad" by engaging in certain risky behaviors. These activities may include smoking, drinking, or sniffing glue for excitement.

One young man, who is quoted in Blum's book, describes the scene:

> *We'd go on a Saturday and see who could sniff the most tubes of glue, man. Didn't even know what to do, dump the glue in a sock, and you know, roll it, and after you start sniffing, it's just something new and you flash. "I'm bad now!"* [1]

The young people who strive to be the "baddest" engage in petty thievery, vandalism, and fighting. Day by day they become more aggressive and assaultive. Gradually, the danger and the need to defend themselves become obvious. The young person, Blum reports, soon learns it is necessary to meet violence with violence. Toughness becomes a goal. "You got to be a rough little dude when you're coming up. You got to be to survive, man."

Groups of so-called dudes, who act and talk tough, grow apart from others their own age. They choose as their role models older children who are insolent and mean. At the same time, they look down their noses at young children whom they consider "punks." They often feel justified venting their anger and aggression on them.

> *You just want to be bad, man; it's in the air. The little dudes around the block, they want to act older than they are, think it's all big and bad to beat up some kid on the street. . . .*[2]

Being a lookout is the entry-level position for nine- and ten-year-olds in the drug trade. It is the job of a lookout to warn dealers when police are in the area. For this, they can make up to $100 a day and be rewarded with a pair of fashionable sneakers, a bomber jacket, or a bicycle.

Becoming part of the drug culture provides kids who have a propensity for violence with exactly the mixture of fear, pleasure, and excitement they crave. Part of their emotional makeup is an attraction toward "messing up." Messing up involves mostly open defiance and clashing with authority figures—everyone from parents to classroom teachers to police officers.

Drug taking at a young age may be quite limited. Yet these early experiences with drugs play a role in developing boldness—the basis for becoming fully involved in the drug trade.

Those who continue along the same path, when they are around twelve to fifteen years old, may become more belligerent in a variety of situations. School truancy and frequent run-ins with the police become more common. Many drop out of school altogether.

According to recent research, the relationship between substance abuse and delinquency may be stronger for school dropouts than for others. For example, among violent delinquents, nearly half are school dropouts. Forty percent report drug use while at school. And dropouts are more likely to have used drugs immediately prior to their violent behaviors.[3]

Being a runner is the next step up the ladder for ambitious young teenagers who want to succeed in the drug trade. The job can pay up to $300 a day. The runner transports the drugs to the dealers on the street. In the case of crack, the youngster takes the drug from the makeshift factories, where cocaine powder is cooked into rock-hard crack, to the dealers.

Many kids growing up in an environment of drugs and violence become involved in terrorizing others. They become increasingly cruel—even vicious. In some neighborhoods, a rowdy group will simply take over street corners and alleys and make them into their private domains. They may provoke fights and otherwise create dangerous situations. The youngsters at this stage are often considered "crazy" in that they do not care about "nothin' and nobody," even, it seems, themselves.

Overall, criminality rises in early adolescence and peaks at sixteen to seventeen years of age. By high school, some drug users have progressed from early experimentation with drugs to the use of major drugs, perhaps barbiturates or amphetamines.

Friends may compete to achieve the most intense drug experience or act in the most outrageous or bizarre manner after drug use.

*It's like you always got to be one step bigger than any-
body else, you know. Like if somebody's drinking beer
you goin' out and get some whiskey. So he's drinking
wine and you go out an' drop some pills. You always
hustling just to show everybody what you can do.*[4]

HUSTLING

Youngsters in the drug culture are often completely on
their own. Family members may be living apart or may
be dead. One young man recently arrested for dealing
told police that he never knew his father, his mother died
a few years ago, and his brother was murdered in a drug
dispute. Seventy-two percent of the boys and girls in a
correctional institute study said they had grown up without one or both parents. About half of those surveyed
said they lived mainly with their mothers. More than half
reported that a close relative had also been imprisoned at
least once.[5]

Experienced drug dealers look for ghetto youngsters
who are eager to make money and who look and act aggressive and violent. Yet, at the same time, many dealers
are wary of those who are too reckless and impulsive,
fearing that such behaviors present too much of a risk to
those who sell drugs in the illegal marketplace.

So far as those dealers are concerned, youngsters who
want to get into the drug market must learn to keep their
"cool." Those who fly off the handle too easily or act too
impulsive may not be listened to and may not be trusted.
Experienced dealers may tend to ignore them and keep
them at a safe distance.

By the time they are sixteen, some youngsters have
disappeared from the drug trade because they have either
died, been imprisoned, or outgrown the lifestyle. A few
succeed in breaking free of the drug culture. An interest
in dating, and the appearance of drug-free models in their
lives, may help this process along. Also, the young per-

son may become concerned about the fact that so many friends and acquaintances are getting killed, going to jail, or leading lives with no future.

For others, though, the passage into drug dependency accelerates, as does the involvement in drug-related crime. The demand for drugs brings a need for pocket money. This need can be satisfied by street-level dealing. The young person finds himself or herself drifting in the direction of hustling. When the opportunity arises, the individual is ready.

The hustling life, beginners learn, takes nerve, cleverness, knowledge, skill, and luck. The game starts to get very tough, competition becomes very keen, and the new hustler must be careful.

As one young hustler said in Dr. Blum's book:

> You got it down to where you don't care about anybody. You're trying to be slick, keeping your game tight, and that's all you care about. You're that cold dude, and nobody's gonna mess with you. Whatever you say, they're gonna jump.[6]

A hustler who wants to remain in the game takes advantage of new opportunities for making money. Often this depends on impressing others with his or her success. This means conspicuous consumption: Cadillacs and Porsches, designer clothes, gold chains, Rolex watches, and $150 Bally shoes. On any given day, young people starting out in the world of drugs wear outfits that may be worth $2,000 or more.

For those who succeed in the hustling world, the illegal drug economy provides a chance to build up the ego and earn a great deal of money. Aggressive young men are generally eager to get to the next step—the status of dealer. They like being part of an in-group—to be looked up to and respected. Dealing gives them a chance to gain the position and power that they view as part of manhood. In a city such as New York, a young dealer can make up to $3,000 a day in the crack trade. Many young dealers also use drug profits to help their families. "They feel like they have to be the breadwinners. It is a manhood thing because there is no father in the house," says a community-action worker.[7]

VIOLENCE AGAINST
AND BY OTHER DEALERS

After selling marijuana and cocaine, starting at age fourteen, Jeff Woodbine (not his real name) saw that drug dealing was the quickest way of making money. He outsold other dealers by offering clients free samples and running two-for-one sales on drugs. As you can imagine, this success brought certain new risks and a need for Jeff to protect himself. He began to carry an automatic pistol and a sawed-off shotgun for protection.

Many user/dealers carry guns for their own protection and to help them handle other dealers. Some dealers who are too young to drive carry such state-of-the-art firearms as Uzi submachine guns, .357 Magnums, and MAC 10s. "You don't see Saturday-night specials anymore," says New York deputy police chief Raymond Kelly. "It's a thing of the past."[8]

Experts find that with all these guns around, many adolescents tend to be trigger-happy. Gang shoot-outs caused 387 deaths in Los Angeles in 1987; more than half the victims were innocent bystanders. "You put a gun in kids' hands, and they are more dangerous than adults," says Janice Warder of the District Attorney's Office in Dallas County, Texas. "They just don't realize the value of life or how easy it is to kill somebody." Wayne County (Michigan) assistant prosecutor Augustus Hutting puts it this way: "Crack, cocaine, guns, and youth are an extremely lethal mixture."[9]

When they fall on hard times, the young hustlers may feel forced to sell their gun for a fix. In this way, some dealers become a conduit for buying and selling guns. It is said that a shrewd dealer can make more money trading guns for drugs than by selling them for cash.

According to Blum:

> *Most of the guns coming into the drug trade come from nickel and dime addicts [$4 and $10 small purchasers] who burgle houses and boost autos. They pick up handguns that way to exchange for heavy narcotics. Nowadays he'll pick guns up here and there until he has five or six. Then he'll go get one or two $50 balloons [heroin]. That dealer will take the guns to his supplier and get about 50 percent more heroin than if he'd paid for it in cash. That supports his habit and gives him a little extra to sell on the side.*[10]

Blum and his associates tried to find out for themselves how the arms-drug exchange worked. In exactly five days after beginning undercover work an associate was offered 400 U.S. Army 45-caliber pistols in return for heroin—showing that drug dealing and arms sales do indeed go together.

A large percentage of those dealers who do not trade in guns still carry arms. One police officer who has made more than 2,000 drug arrests in six years states that over 95 percent of those nabbed carried weapons—about half were guns and the other half illegal knives with concealed blades over 3 inches (7.6 cm) long.

Armed dealers have longer histories of arrests for drug use and/or nondrug crimes than unarmed dealers. Also, they have many more convictions for using weapons to steal drugs from other dealers, distributors, and users. Most like to think of themselves as professional dealers and criminals. Their backgrounds tend to be lower-class, uneducated, and from broken homes. They are heavy drug users who live with the constant fear that someone is going to hurt them.

Authorities report increasingly brutal and bizarre crimes committed by young dealers. In Detroit, boys as young as fourteen have been locked up for torturing fellow dealers. Youngsters reportedly have given powerful electric shocks to their victims and poured alcohol on open wounds. Young dealers who run teenage crack houses often make pornographic videotapes of activities going on in their houses. "A lot of it is group sex," says Sergeant Elmer Harris, a Detroit police officer, "or inducing girls to have sex with each other or with dogs."[11]

Adolescent crack dealers who sell drugs to children are cruel and immoral. Crack has proved the most seductive drug for children. A child can get a vial of crack for $3 to $5. A dealer can make hundreds of vials from a couple of grams, and for the addict one $3 vial leads to another and another and another. Some young addicts are known to have stolen $700 and spent it all smoking crack for one day. The high is instantaneous, the addiction just as fast. One Detroit drug rehabilitation program treats children as young as six years old!

Curiously enough, the most successful young crack dealers are usually bright and articulate. They understand how to keep track of the money they earn and they know how to run their business. But the price they pay for this so-called success is a life full of crime and brutality. Few see their life continuing much beyond the present.

PROSTITUTION

Drug use may not be costly to begin with, but ultimately, the young person must begin to pay for his or her habit. Generally this means resorting to drug dealing. It may also involve resorting to other illegal means if dealing fails to provide enough money. Some young men and women turn from dealing to prostitution as a means of supporting their drug habits.

One recent example illustrates this shift from drug dealing to prostitution to pay for drugs. A sixteen-year-old mother with a two-year-old child was living in a public housing project struggling to cover rent and food expenses on a small weekly budget. Her boyfriend offered to pay her $300 to $400 a night for selling customers $20 packets of cocaine wrapped in aluminum foil. Her income mounted, and for a while she was very pleased with herself. But the money gradually began to disappear into her own growing cocaine habit. One night the police staged a raid, and her friend was arrested. Although she was not caught, she had only a few dollars left in savings. She needed more cocaine. The next day she took to the streets in search of men who would pay her to sleep with them.

Many prostitutes, like the young woman just cited, first sold drugs as their source of income. They became involved with prostitution when they lost their source of supply because their "connection" was arrested or killed by another dealer or user. Others were forced out of the drug trade when they were caught skimming or selling phony drugs. A few lost their clientele because they were suspected of being police informants. Or, finally, they may have resorted to prostitution because selling drugs was not profitable enough.

In *The War on Drugs*, James A. Inciardi quotes a female prostitute:

> All of a sudden there's nothin' out there on the streets—nothin' to sell or buy either. How can you make a living on the street dealin' if there's nothin' anywhere to deal? [12]

Research by Inciardi indicates that most of the prostitutes on drugs experienced considerable violence in their lives, both as victims and perpetrators. Many who were on heroin or other drugs, he writes, supplemented their incomes periodically by assaulting and robbing, or secretly stealing from, their clients. Of the over 25,000 instances of prostitution, one in seven also involved a theft or robbery. Also, the female prostitutes who were on drugs tended to commit more crimes and be more violent than those who were drug-free.[13]

Among those who support their drug habits by prostitution are many victims who have contracted AIDS from their sexual partners. The life style is also pervaded with violence. Alice, for instance, sells herself to truckers who use a highway just north of the fifth-floor crack den she shares with a couple she met at reform school and a number of other girls. The young woman has been living there since being thrown out on the street by her alcoholic mother. When the crack runs out, there are often violent arguments and fights over whether someone smoked more than his or her share. Girls such as Alice, some as young as fourteen, are often beaten by other crack addicts. Alice has been raped three times and been repeatedly beaten and robbed.

The data seems to suggest that, in many cases, major drug use preceded prostitution. But Inciardi argues that drug use has little if anything to do with a career in prostitution. Most prostitutes, he finds, had criminal careers before they experimented with drugs. He believes that the general circumstances of their social and economic situation may have more to do with leading people to become prostitutes than the fact that they are taking drugs.

STREET CRIME

In many cities, drug use, particularly crack, pervades the daily life of many inhabitants. The never-ending search for money to buy drugs provides the motives for countless muggings, burglaries, and robberies. The addicts, most of whom are young, prey on storekeepers, honest working people, children, and the elderly to support their drug habits. Poor, inner-city neighborhoods are especially hard-hit by this violence.

The victims of drug-related street crime are often drunks or loners—people with money in their pockets who are not fully aware of the dangers around them or who are not known in the community. Nat Wilson, age fifty-nine, lives in a homeless shelter where drugs are rampant. He said that he arrived at the shelter with a few hundred dollars in a pouch tied to a string around his neck. The very first night someone stole the pouch and money while he was asleep![14]

Another man said he had been robbed three times within several weeks in the shelter. In one incident, several men jumped him in bed and cut through his pants pocket to get at his money, he said. According to one shelter official, on most days at least one serious drug-related fight and several muggings come to the attention of the staff; many others are never reported.

On February 3, 1988, less than a month past his thirteenth birthday, James Watkins was stabbed fourteen times in what the police called a drug-related robbery. The boy, who survived the assault, was carrying $1,000 in cash and some crack when he was attacked. The three teenagers who were later arrested for the crime admitted that they knew that James had a lot of money on him and attacked him when they knew he was likely to be alone. James learned how to hustle when he was about eight, his father said. "He was hustling to make some money. Maybe he was holding it for somebody."[15]

In one of the most terrible juvenile crime sprees in New York City history, a seventeen-year-old crack addict robbed and shot five people in less than six hours on January 1, 1988. The next day, he went out again after dark and robbed three stores. At the first store, the teenager took cash but shot no one. He stole about $80 from the second store and shot four people, two of whom died. A child was shot during the third robbery at a food market. The teen continued this violent rampage of robberies and shooting for two more days, until he was finally captured by the police. According to the police, the motive for all this violence was to obtain money for crack![16]

CONCLUSION

Because most drug dealers are also users, it is often difficult to tell where one role begins and the other leaves off. Their behavior when under the influence of drugs or withdrawing from them, and their pursuit of drugs or the money to purchase them all become part of a dangerous and violent life pattern.

About one of every three addicts arrested is charged with both sale *and* possession. The obvious explanation is that drugs lend themselves to small-scale dealing and are also a quick, though extremely hazardous, way to raise cash to obtain drugs. As a source of income, dealing is especially attractive to low-income, disadvantaged youth. With few other possibilities for employment and troubling family situations, many embark on a career of drug dealing. Invariably the careers are violent, short-lived, and interrupted by short or long stays in correctional institutions.

Violence and incarceration among street dealers is inevitable when you consider the basic facts: The dealers are trading in expensive and illegal products. They are operating outside the protection of the law and other safeguards of society. They are often cheated and robbed in the course of their work, and they in turn steal from their fellow drug users and dealers. Their ownership of guns and other weapons adds to the considerable tensions that already exist. And of course, they are constantly vulnerable to capture or arrest by law-enforcement officers.

While some make money in low-level drug peddling, many are not content to deal on this level. They seek greater profits. To earn it they become exceptionally well organized, engage in very tough business practices, and take especially high risks—characteristics of middle-level dealing, our next topic.

CHAPTER

MIDDLE-LEVEL DRUG DEALING AND VIOLENCE

- *Police Officer Edward Byrne was killed by three bullets fired into his head at close range while guarding a witness in a drug case. The slaying was directed by drug dealers seeking retaliation for their arrest by the police.*

- *On a hot summer night in 1988, police were called to a shooting scene where they found two people wounded and a twenty-two-year-old man dead. The same weapon had been used in an attack ten minutes earlier and less than a mile away, where six people were hurt and a seventeen-year-old boy was killed. The shootings were part of a drug-turf war between rival gangs.*

- *A four-year-old boy was critically injured when he was caught in an exchange of gunfire between two gangs arguing over drugs.*

- *Five drug-gang members who set out to avenge a drug deal gone wrong allegedly shot down two innocent young women in a case of mistaken identity.*

- *Sixty-three automatic rifles and forty handguns were seized by federal authorities in raids on Chinese gangs accused of traf-*

ficking in heroin and guns. Twenty-four people were arrested and over 112 pounds (51 kg) of heroin were seized.

■ *Two federal drug agents were shot to death in an undercover drug operation. They had been carrying $90,000 to buy from a trafficker 2 pounds (0.9 kg) of heroin to be used as evidence.*

Murders, kidnappings, fire bombings, and death threats are part of the violence in the drug trade in cities across the United States. At the center of all the violence are the so-called drug kingpins. These are mid-level dealers who come from the streets and earn up to $10,000 a night from the drug trade.

Any number of drug rings and gangs vie to control the street drug trade. These modern-day hoodlums and gangsters fight wars over territory, steal from and kill one another, and keep their members in line with threats, beatings, and bullets. Not only do they inflict terrible violence on each other, but they ruin and destroy many innocent lives in the process.

STREET-CORNER CARTELS

Drugs are routinely sold in tens of thousands of places in all parts of the country. But it was the spread of crack that led to the street-corner cartels and major dealers such as Lorenzo (Fat Cat) Nichols. (His nickname may have come from a onetime weight problem.) Nichols is a good example of someone who worked his way up from low- to mid-level dealing. But he also represents a dying breed. New gangs on the street are now challenging the old bosses.

Born on Christmas Day in 1958, Lorenzo Nichols grew up in a southeast Queens neighborhood in New York City. While in his teens he joined a local gang of older men and began robbing stores. On the street, he was thought of as "tough," ready to use his fists and guns, and good at intimidating people. By seventeen he had been arrested four times for weapons possession and larceny. After being convicted of holding up a bar at gunpoint, he was sentenced to two and a half years in prison.

Nichols was released from prison in 1980 and put on parole. Shortly afterward, he set about organizing a drug-distribution business. He formed an alliance with some other cocaine dealers and sold $10 and $20 bags of heroin and cocaine from six outlets in the metropolitan area. He supervised an organization of some twenty "executive officers," "lieutenants," "comptrollers," and "security people." Nichols ran a tight operation, with quick murder of competitors—some of whom he burned to death with gasoline.

In the summer of 1985, twenty police officers raided Nichols's headquarters and found him there with five associates. Nichols had in his possession two loaded automatic weapons and a 9-mm 18-shot automatic. The police also found 6 ounces (170 g) of cocaine, several pounds of marijuana, scales, a money-counting machine, and $180,000 in cash. Since Nichols had violated the terms of his release from prison, he was arrested. His parole officer, Brian Rooney, testified against him.

Two months later, Rooney was killed. The murderer allegedly was Nichols's "enforcer," Howard Mason. Sources claimed that Fat Cat had offered Mason $5,000 to kill Rooney.

From jail, Nichols continued to operate his business. He learned that the situation in his territory was changing. Although older dealers continued to control part of the cocaine and heroin trade, the whole neighborhood was turning to crack. Young crack sellers were cutting into his area and his profits.

The crack dealers were hurting Nichols in other ways, too. On May 16, 1987, rival dealers kidnapped José Verella, a cocaine dealer linked to Nichols. After Verella's father refused to pay ransom for José, he was shot. Two weeks later, another Nichols associate was also murdered. Then Fat Cat's wife, Joanne, was taken hostage. She was released only after Nichols's father produced $80,000 in cash as ransom.

In the fall of 1987, the government tried its case against Nichols for large-scale drug trafficking, and he was sentenced to twenty-five years to life in prison. A week later, Police Officer Edward Byrne was fatally shot in Nichols's territory. The order to kill the officer was believed to have come from Nichols.[1]

Police have had a difficult time investigating this crime because the borough of Queens, where the incident occurred, has ten or more groups vying for turf. Precisely who is in what group and what the relationships are between the various drug-dealing enterprises is often hard to tell. Alliances shift and new as well as would-be operators come along frequently.

At the time of the shooting, the neighborhood where Officer Byrne was slain had become the territory of Thomas (Mustaffa) Godbolt, who was either an associate of Fat Cat Nichols or was operating there with Fat Cat's permission. Officer Byrne was killed while guarding the home of a man named Arjune, a government witness who had been threatened by Godbolt.

Godbolt, who had been convicted of criminal weapons possession in 1982, was awaiting trial for having threatened Arjune. But even though Godbolt had a motive in killing Officer Byrne, the police did not have evidence to make an arrest. Instead, a federal complaint was filed on August 12, 1988, finding the entire Nichols organization responsible for the Byrne killing.[2] On March 29, 1989, three drug dealers were convicted of the murder of Officer Byrne.

GANG WARFARE

The arrival of crack opened the drug market to new traffickers, who bought cocaine for a few hundred dollars, manufactured it into crack, and sold it on the street at a great profit. The result was a level of competition unheard of among traditional drug traffickers, and the rise of crack gangs.

Most crack gangs are alike in several ways. They range in size from six to thirty people, with most members in their teens to mid-twenties. Each group seeks to control a specific area. To demonstrate their toughness, the gangs normally kill in daylight and often on crowded streets. The gunmen prefer shooting a victim in the head at close range without attempting to disguise their identities.[3]

Experts say that these young crack-gang dealers play by different rules than did the older drug dealers. Most of today's mid-level dealers come from violent homes and have violent backgrounds. They have but one thought: to get rich quick. Their actions are not restrained by any code of behavior or by any feelings of loyalty. Their actions are highly unpredictable because many not only peddle drugs but also use them. Apprehending and arresting these dealers is extremely difficult and dangerous for the police.[4]

Jamaican dealers have been in the crack business since it first was introduced in the United States in the mid-1980s. Known as *posses*, the Jamaican gangs are independently organized and very violent. They do not hesitate to kill rivals to get the best spots to sell drugs and attract the best customers. Often, they will rob other dealers to build up their supply. And they will give merciless beatings to any *posse* members who hold back money or try to cheat the gang in any other way. According to government sources, there are thirty to forty *posses* with a total of about 5,000 members now operating in the U.S.[5]

Nationwide, the Jamaican gangs have been linked to 800 murders, including more than 350 in 1987 alone! *Posse* gunmen generally prefer shooting their victims in public. A dispute between *posse* members at a reggae club in Houston led to a fatal shooting in front of nearly a hundred witnesses. New York police report that homicides occur almost weekly at one popular nightspot known as the Love People disco. Torture and maimings are *posse* trademarks as well.

Twenty-nine-year-old Delroy Edwards, one of the most feared Jamaican crack organizers in the United States, was arrested in March 1988. Police said Mr. Edwards's *posses* obtained "kilogram quantities of cocaine . . . by robbing cocaine dealers." Those dealers who did not turn over the drugs were murdered or assaulted. In November 1986 Edwards shot three men in the legs because one of them was missing $500 from his day's drug receipts.[6]

Traditional crime organizations usually exercise tight control and discipline *only* within their own group. However, says Thomas Moyer, an expert on Jamaican *posses*, the Jamaicans are trying to intimidate everyone. They seem to have little regard for the sanctity of human life. Many make a point of staging their assassinations in broad daylight and fire point-blank. "You don't kill . . . from across the street," one young hitman explained to undercover agents. "You walk up to him, you kill him in his head."[7]

As a result of their violent policies, the Jamaicans have achieved great influence in the drug market. They have more control over the packaging and sale of cocaine than most other drug dealers in the United States. "They get it, cut it, and run it, controlling the distribution all the way down to the street level," says Moyer.

In some cities, where the Jamaicans have not yet taken over, the distribution network is dominated by other organized groups. The Los Angeles market, for example, is controlled by local gangs. With about 600 gangs in the area, Los Angeles County is often referred to as the gang capital of the nation. The desperate poverty in the poor areas of the city and the huge amounts of money that can be made by selling crack combine to give the gangs extraordinary power.

Most of the Los Angeles gangs are black or Hispanic, but there are Asian, Samoan, and Caucasian ones, as well. There are about 70,000 gang members, including the "wannabees" and "gonnabees." These are preadolescent boys awaiting initiation, which sometimes requires a drive-by murder. Such murders are usually random events, with no motive at all, committed from the window of a moving car. During the first four months of 1988, there were 109 gang-related killings in Los Angeles County; many of the victims were innocent bystanders.[8]

The black gangs are by far the most violent of the Los Angeles gangs. Their 25,000 or so members are usually heavily armed. Hispanic gangs tend to fight mostly over turf; they pose more of a danger to one another than to outsiders.

The two best-known names among Los Angeles gangs are the Bloods and the Crips. They are, however, loose confederations—as opposed to tightly organized gangs—of hundreds of subgroups, or "sets." Sets are formed along neighborhood lines; and most have between twenty and a hundred members. Bloods wear red and Crips wear blue; traditionally, each gang member wears or carries a bandanna (his "rag") to show his colors.

Experts say the big-city gangs are spreading the drug trade all over the United States. Because of the glut of drugs in California, some Los Angeles gangs have moved out from their home base to the smaller cities and towns of the West. The result has been a rise in violence in these new areas as the gangs fight each other for a share of the market.

The Los Angeles gangs have also begun to spread farther east. They have penetrated into several Midwestern cities that, until recently, had little history of cocaine use. In some places, such as Kansas City, California gangs moved in to fill the vacuum created by police action against the Jamaican gangs in late 1988.

When gang members set out to take over the drug action in a city, they behave like very shrewd, sophisticated business people. They make their presence known in a new city by driving luxury cars and flaunting expensive jewelry and clothing. To get a toehold in the new territory, they offer free samples and try to undersell their competitors. Because they are able to buy top-quality cocaine from major smugglers at wholesale prices, they offer better deals on both price and quality to drug users. And, as if these advantages were not enough, they intimidate the competition with violence, mayhem, and murder.

V. G. Guinses, director of a California agency that works to reduce the level of gang violence, says the gangs "have decided to do what the Kentucky Colonel and McDonald's have done: open franchises."[9] In Seattle, which had virtually no gang members in 1986, the police attributed 167 major crimes between early 1987 and early 1988 to local gangs operating under the control of established gangs in Los Angeles and elsewhere.[10]

In St. Louis, gang members are just starting to establish themselves. Denver already has an estimated 700 gang members. Omaha now has a crack problem that it never had before. Robert Armstrong, director of the Omaha Housing Authority, put it this way: "These people have no fear. Whether they are Crips or Crips imitators, they sell their drugs anytime they feel like selling. And they intimidate the police by letting them know they have guns."[11]

Behind the scenes, much of the ghetto cocaine trade is controlled by so-called O.G.'s, short for "old gangsters." These are individuals who have made it big in the drug trade. They are near the top of the distribution pyramid. For instance, an estimated fifteen to twenty O.G.'s control the entire cocaine trade in south-central Los Angeles.

Meanwhile, other big-city gangs in New York, Chicago, Miami, and Washington, ply the crack business as well. In Chicago, gang membership has now reached an estimated 13,000. A Miami-based gang called the Untouchables is believed to be selling crack as far north as

Atlanta, Savannah, and other cities of the Southeast. In these places, the group is known as the Miami Boys. In Atlanta alone, says Police Lieutenant John Woodward, the invading Miami Boys caused thirteen homicides in 1987.[12]

Since the beginning of 1988, Washington, D.C.'s crime rate has been climbing as local peddlers continue to violently clash with Jamaican dealers from New York and Miami. According to Washington police chief Maurice Turner, Jr., the violence will subside when the warriors decide how to divide up the drug trade. Nevertheless, statistics showed a 100 percent increase in homicides, nearly 80 percent of which are drug-related.[13]

In recent years, there has been a gradual change in patterns of gang violence. Before, most gang conflicts were battles over turf, or territory. Now, in addition, there is an increased use of violence in the day-to-day running of drug operations. Users who don't pay their bills, dealers who steal, cheat, or lie, and all those suspected of informing to the police are ruthlessly punished by anything from a beating to a bullet.

One of the most powerful of the big-city drug gangs, the Chambers brothers, was dismantled by the Detroit police in late 1988. The Chambers brothers' organization had clawed its way to the top and controlled over half of all the crack houses in Detroit, with sales calculated at $1 to $3 million a day! With hundreds of employees, the ring completely dominated the drug trade in large areas of Detroit. At the time the four Chambers brothers were arrested, the Detroit Police Department seized $1 million in cash and jewelry, sixty-eight automobiles, 250 weapons, and 6 kilograms (over 13 lb) of cocaine.

Dr. Carl Taylor is an adjunct professor of criminal justice at Michigan State University and an expert on youth gangs. He described the Chambers gang as having had a corporate organization. Equipped with a very tight structure and specific bylaws, they made harsh demands on their hundreds of employees, many of whom were high school students. These youngsters were paid $100 a day to skip school and work twelve-hour shifts selling or preparing the crack.

To obtain cheap, dependable labor the brothers lured scores of young people to Detroit from the Chambers brothers' original hometown, Marianna, Arkansas. Instead of having to work hard in the rice and soybean fields for low wages, young men were given $2,000 a month to work in Detroit as runners and dealers. "They [the Chambers brothers] were like slave traders, bringing kids up from the south and locking them in these crack houses," said Dr. Taylor.[14]

The Chambers brothers threatened and abused the young men to keep them in line. Youths caught sampling the cocaine were beaten. The punishments for stealing could be harsh. One Marianna boy returned home with his fingers brutally broken and mangled. To maintain control, the brothers would sometimes deliberately cheat the street-level dealers in the amount of crack they were given to sell. When the receipts came up short, the boys were blamed and were forced to work off their shortages; this kept them in perpetual bondage.

But not all the brutality of the gang leaders was directed at the workers. Arguments and rivalries between the Southern recruits and the Detroit workers led to many fights, shootings, and at least four murders.

It is unclear what will happen now that the Chambers brothers have been jailed. The workers that are left may be forming their own gangs to fill the void in Detroit. At the same time, new groups are probably organizing to get some part of the action.

Meanwhile, some of the former employees are believed to have returned to Marianna and taken their drug know-how with them. Young men who left as so-called country bumpkins are returning as experienced drug dealers and hardened criminals.

Many people are concerned that the Chambers brothers will be able to continue their violent ways, even from inside prison. The ones in greatest danger are those who testified against them and those who are trying to take over their territory. Already there have been several fire bombings, including one directed against a woman who was witness in the Chambers brothers' trial.

REPRISALS
AGAINST WITNESSES

"There have always been killings in the drug business, but these gangs believe that if they can intimidate everybody, they can operate openly and flourish," said William K. Hoyt, Jr., head of New York City's homicide unit.[15] Since 1984 the homicide unit has solved fewer than 10 percent of gang killings. Although the unit convicted seventeen gang members of twenty-one slayings, according to Hoyt, those found guilty are "conservatively suspected of having killed at least double the number of cases we brought them to trial for." Most drug-gang homicides may be unsolvable because witnesses fear retaliation against themselves or their families if they testify against the gang members.

Residents in neighborhoods where drug dealers flourish see the dealers taking over their lives and communities, bit by bit. The dealers keep children away from playgrounds and park areas. They take over empty apartments and the lobbies, halls, and stairways of apartment buildings. Fights and arguments that break out among drug dealers quickly escalate into gun battles, often with automatic weapons. For fear of being injured or killed by a stray bullet, residents are virtual prisoners in their own homes and children are not allowed to go anywhere but school.

Not long ago, two women, Ella Jones and Melva Doyle, embarked on a campaign to drive drug dealers from their apartment complex in Stockton, California. The women confronted the gangs and threatened to call the police. In April 1988 one of the women's car windows was shot out. She later reported, "They [the dealers] told my girls they were going to get me because I was a snitch."[16]

But such instances of standing up to drug dealers are rare. Most residents are completely intimidated. So much fear exists that it is almost impossible to find a witness willing to testify in a gang-related crime case, according to detectives. Many remember the example of Mildred Green, a sixty-one-year-old taxi dispatcher, who was shot to death in October 1988 shortly after informing a grand jury about a shoot-out she had witnessed between suspected drug dealers.[17]

A more publicized attempt to silence a witness was the violence waged against the Guyanese immigrant named Arjune, who was mentioned before. Arjune had moved into a Queens, New York, neighborhood with his family in September 1987. The formerly vacant house was situated on a very active, very profitable street corner for local drug dealers. The drug dealers were furious with Arjune when his complaints led to the arrest of three of the dealers. Arjune also agreed to testify against them, which increased the drug dealers' displeasure.

Hours after the arrest of the three dealers, someone threw a fire bomb through a first-floor window of Arjune's house, causing minor damage. As the police were arresting a young man for the attack, a second fire bomb was flung through Arjune's window. Later, Police Officer Edward Byrne was fatally shot while guarding the house. No doubt, Arjune's experiences and the murder of Mildred Green make other eyewitnesses reluctant to report drug crimes or help prosecute the perpetrators.

VIOLENCE AGAINST INNOCENT BYSTANDERS

Scores of innocent bystanders have been killed in drug wars. Some just had the bad luck to be walking or driving nearby during a gun battle. Others were victims of "drive-by" shootings that happened as they stood chatting with neighbors, walking a grandchild, or playing ball in an area claimed as drug-sales territory by rival gangs.

A few illustrations: In May 1988, three drug-gang members began wildly firing their guns, probably trying to frighten rival drug distributors or warn away neighborhood drug users. Of the fifteen shots they fired, one passed through a first-floor window, through a bed headboard, and struck Rosa Urena, twenty, as she lay sleeping. The next day the young woman was declared brain dead.[18]

On August 19, 1988, one person was killed and eight others—seven of them bystanders—were wounded in two separate shooting incidents near their homes in New York City. The shootings, one of which involved an M-16 automatic rifle, appeared to have been products of a turf war between crack merchants.

Over one weekend in September 1988, shotgun blasts in drive-by shootings by drug-gang thugs killed one man and wounded his companion, a bystander, and two members of a different gang.

Two men, believed to be gang members, were booked on charges of attempted murder after opening fire on a crowd at a hamburger stand. Officers who were watching the stand because of two other recent drive-by shootings saw several people limp away after the attack, but nobody reported an injury to the authorities and no one volunteered to testify.

José Vasquez was playing basketball in his housing project when he was hit in the leg by a shotgun blast fired from a passing van. Police speculated that the shooting may have been related to tenants' complaints about pervasive drug trafficking in the area.[19]

Authorities believe that street violence is part of the rapid escalation in drug trafficking, especially by out-of-town dealers in cocaine and crack. The situation often occurs when drug dealers move into new areas pushing drugs.

CONCLUSION

Young and violent drug gangs are presently engaged in brutal territorial battles and calculated campaigns to terrorize neighborhoods. The gangs seek to eliminate rivals, discourage informers, and keep law-abiding residents from complaining about open drug sales on city streets.

New law-enforcement approaches have put some very dangerous people in prison. These people probably would have committed more murders and mayhem if police had not been able to disrupt the activities of these mid-level drug-distributing networks. However, much of the violence that takes place is caused by drug traffickers at the top of the drug-trade pyramid. In the next chapter, we will consider the violent rivalries that rage among these major drug distributors.

CHAPTER

TOP-LEVEL DRUG TRAFFICKING AND VIOLENCE

- *Two drug organizations, the Pagans and the Bruno drug family, agreed to divide the amphetamine and PCP markets in different American cities and to stop competing with one another. The street value of the Pagans' PCP and amphetamine operations was estimated at $15.5 million.*

- *The seventeen-month-long so-called pizza-connection trial charged twenty-two defendants with operating a $1.65-billion Sicilian Mafia heroin ring. One government witness admitted committing thirteen contract killings.*

- *A federal drug agent was kidnapped, tortured, and finally killed on a ranch in Mexico. The men charged with his murder were part of a large drug-trafficking operation that the agent had uncovered and was investigating.*

- *The explosion of a car bomb killed two security guards in front of a luxury apartment building owned by Colombia's reputed billionaire cocaine czar. The drug lord escaped unharmed.*

Large-scale drug trafficking is considered the most serious organized-crime problem in the world today. Sales of cocaine, heroin, and marijuana account for nearly 40 percent of the activities of such groups. They are said to generate an annual income as high as $110 billion![1]

Not only does drug trafficking produce billions of dollars for organized crime each year, but the huge distribution networks impose much hardship, pain, and suffering on individuals, families, communities, and governments everywhere. Despite efforts to halt the flood of drug supplies, traffickers have never before been as rich, powerful, and ruthless.

THE PROBLEM

Leading the large trafficking organizations that dominate the illicit drug market are the crime families of the United States' La Cosa Nostra. In addition, there are several more-recently identified crime groups, such as the Sicilian Mafia, and groups based in Nigerian and Colombian communities around the United States. Although La Cosa Nostra has historically been involved in narcotics trafficking, these newer organizations—in many ways quite different—now play a significant role in the drug trade.

The newer groups differ from La Cosa Nostra in a few ways. They have developed solely around drug-trafficking operations and depend completely on drug-related criminal activity for income. They tend to be more loosely organized than La Cosa Nostra. They are not as self-contained. And, perhaps most important, the new drug organizations surpass La Cosa Nostra in the amount of violence and corruption present in all aspects of their criminal activity.

COCAINE TRAFFICKING
AND VIOLENCE

Control of the cocaine industry has traditionally been maintained by a cartel of Colombian traffickers. They are the largest, wealthiest, and most sophisticated suppliers of cocaine in the world.

The cultivation, preparation, and transportation required to bring cocaine from the fields of South America to the streets of the United States obviously depends on good organization. The major Colombian traffickers carefully control each step of the process.

The American cocaine supply presently originates mostly in South America, from the leaves of the coca bush. The plant is grown principally by Peruvian or Bolivian peasants in remote areas of the eastern Andes and is processed into cocaine in nearby villages. The growers are allied in small, independent groups. These groups are typically financed, overseen, and protected by members of a larger organization from Colombia.

The plants are first harvested as early as eighteen months after planting. From then on they can usually be harvested from three to four times annually for up to twenty years. The cultivation of coca has increased significantly in recent years, primarily as a result of the planting of new coca plants and the maturation of existing coca plants.

Organized laborers and processors prepare the cocaine for U.S. consumption. In a relatively simple chemical process, coca leaves are converted in several steps into cocaine hydrochloride, the form of cocaine most commonly abused in this country.

The first step in the conversion process usually occurs near the cultivation site. The partially processed leaves are then smuggled out of the mountain villages of Peru and Bolivia on light aircraft or boats to Colombia, where most of their refining takes place.

Pilots of the Colombian organization land the planes at secret airstrips, often simple dirt runways, located near the processing labs. Approximately 300 kilograms, or "kilos" (660 lb), of coca leaves are needed to produce 1 kilo (2.2 lb) of pure cocaine.[2]

The Colombia cocaine factories take in an estimated 31 million kilos (about 68 million lb) of coca leaves a year and produce about 100,000 kilos (220,500 lb) of pure cocaine. Each step in the manufacturing process reduces the amount of the product, but each step in the distribution process increases it. One kilo "cut" with lactose powder is sold to a distributor as 2 kilos (4.4 lb), 50 percent pure. The distributor cuts it again to produce 4 kilos (8.8 lb), and the dealer turns that into 8 kilos (17.6 lb). At the end, $625 worth of coca leaves in Peru is worth $560,000 on the streets of America![3]

Like traditional organized-crime groups, the Colombian trafficking cartels are built of interdependent divisions, each with a specialized area of responsibility. These organizations often hire experienced criminals to perform various jobs for them.

Because importing cocaine is illegal throughout the world, shipping cocaine across national boundaries is the most developed branch of the industry. The transportation requires an extensive network of alternative routes and methods of shipment. At the same time, the system must be flexible; traffic patterns must be changed often to evade law-enforcement authorities.

Cocaine destined for south Florida, the main point of entry into the United States, and New York, the next most common port, is usually shipped in bundles of several hundred kilos. Most often the bundles are placed inside commercial aircraft and, to a lesser extent, aboard noncommercial craft. Generally, shipments are smuggled out of Colombia from the country's northern coastal region, La Guajira Peninsula. Principal smuggling centers include the cities of Santa Marta, Cartagena, and Medellín.[4]

Colombian trafficking organizations, like other organized-crime groups, rely on enforcement through violence and intimidation. Enforcers protect their inventory and profits both in Colombia and the United States. They collect debts owed to the organization and eliminate competitors, informants, and law-enforcement officials.

Traffickers do not hesitate to assassinate anyone who stands in their way. As *Washington Post* columnist Jack Anderson wrote in September 1988, "57 judges and 250 journalists have been murdered because they got in the cartel's way."[5]

During the 1970s, cocaine traffickers operated throughout Colombia with little interference. In fact, they had considerable support from the Colombian government. The situation changed in April 1984 when drug traffickers assassinated Colombia's minister of justice, Rodrigo Lara Bonilla. His killing came two months after he authorized a raid on a major cocaine-processing plant, known as Tranquilandia, in southeast Colombia. The raid resulted in the destruction of over $1 billion worth of cocaine.

Following Lara's assassination, Colombian president Belisario Betancur Cuartas took strong action. He declared a "war without quarter" on all drug smugglers and signed extradition orders for a number of known major traffickers. As a result, many of the bigger traffickers went into hiding. Several moved their processing operations to neighboring countries.

Medellín cartel leaders, accompanied by nearly a hundred bodyguards, moved to Panama. They paid the country's military leader, General Manuel Antonio Noriega, "four to five million dollars for their protection," according to Floyd Carlton, a former pilot and intermediary between the Medellín leaders and General Noriega.[6] In Mexico, the Medellín traffickers established ties with Mexican drug-trafficking organizations. The relationship led to a surge in cocaine shipments through Mexico.

In June 1987, under the shadow of death threats, the Colombian Supreme Court backed away from a 1979 extradition treaty between Washington and Bogotá. They said it was unconstitutional. Six months later, a major trafficker was released from jail after serving just thirty-nine days on minor charges. Also, Carlos Mauro Hoyos, the Colombian attorney general, was murdered in January 1988. The actions thoroughly demoralized Colombian opponents of the drug traffickers.

In mid-1988, John C. Lawn, administrator of the federal Drug Enforcement Administration (DEA), was asked about the prospects for bringing the leaders of the Medellín cartel to trial. He said the chances were dim. "The judges are saying to us, 'Either we accept money or we are killed,' " Mr. Lawn said. "That doesn't leave much of an option."[7] One Colombian judge tearfully told U.S. authorities that the narco-gangsters had threatened to kill her parents and her children—and she believed that they would![8]

Because the Colombian drug trade is so lucrative, the cartel can afford to spend millions on bribes. Cocaine kingpins, Anderson reports, approach authorities with offers that are hard to refuse—"ploma o plato," "lead or silver," or, in other words, "a bullet or a bribe."[9] Dazzling sums have also been offered to American law-enforcement officials. These huge amounts of money represent attempts to undermine law-enforcement efforts across the United States.

One of the Medellín leaders, Pablo Escobar Gaviria, thirty-nine, specializes in "security" for the organization. Drug-intelligence agents say his organization employs as many as 200 gunmen and at least two "schools for assassins." In these schools, killers are trained, among other things, to shoot victims from the backs of motorbikes.[10] Colombian justice minister Rodrigo Bonilla, who fought the Medellín drug cartel, was gunned down by just such a hit-and-run assassin, who sped away on a motorbike.[11]

The Medellín traffickers remain the most powerful and wealthy cocaine lords in the world. They control 80 percent of all cocaine entering the United States. Yet they have competition from other groups. Another cartel, known as the Cali group, presently poses a real threat.

Between 1987 and 1988, more than a dozen Colombian nationals were murdered in the United States as a result of the conflict between these two organizations. The Cali group reportedly sent more than ten professional killers from Colombia to the United States. Their task was to establish control over hundreds of millions of dollars in sales in New York and other cities.

Robert M. Stutman, special agent in charge of the DEA office in New York, was himself the target of a death threat from a Medellín leader. He says the struggle between the two drug organizations can be expected to result in more planned assassinations and violence. "Both [organizations] have in the past hired gangs of professional assassins," says Mr. Stutman, "and neither of [them] particularly cares who gets caught in the middle."[12]

HEROIN TRAFFICKING
AND VIOLENCE

Heroin is an extremely valuable commodity for organized crime. Surely the fact that an ounce of pure heroin is worth about ten times more than an ounce of gold has something to do with it!

Heroin users provide organized crime with billions of dollars in profits every year. It is estimated that the illegal income from heroin sales in the United States totals approximately $6.12 billion.[13]

Heroin, a narcotic, is derived from the poppy plant, a type of opium. The poppy grows mainly in Southeast Asia, Southwest Asia, and Mexico. The production of the drug begins after the petals of the flower have fallen off. In one method, the sap is taken from the pod and scraped out. This dried sap is raw opium. A chemical is added to the opium, and the mixture is pressed to make a morphine base. Adding another chemical to the morphine produces heroine. Like cocaine, heroin production usually begins at or near the site of cultivation.

Heroin trafficking in this country became big business in the late 1930s. At that time, La Cosa Nostra began to take control of the importation of the drug from France, Asia, and the Mideast. When these sources became inaccessible during World War II, Mexico became the major supplier of heroin to the United States.

After the war, La Cosa Nostra gained complete control of the American heroin market, importing most of the heroin from Italian refineries. When the Italian government banned the manufacture of heroin in the early 1950s, a new system was devised. Incompletely prepared heroin was shipped form Turkey to Marseilles, where it was refined into pure heroin. The heroin was sent to Montreal or Sicily. From there it was smuggled directly into the United States. This arrangement was popularly known as the "French Connection." It allowed La Cosa Nostra to monopolize the heroin trade from the 1960s through the early 1970s, when the French Connection collapsed.

In 1977, Mexico became the major source of U.S. heroin. Mexico has captured an even greater share of the American market with "Black Tar," a crude but potent form of heroin. In high demand, especially in the western United States, Black Tar is cheaper and purer than the usual brown heroin powder.

Violence is an integral part of Mexican heroin trafficking. Traffickers provide the growers and cultivators with semiautomatic and automatic weapons to protect their crops. Weapons are also freely used to eliminate informants and to intimidate competitors and law-enforcement officials. Corruption among Mexican police officials is well documented. It insures the smooth operation of the Mexican trafficking organization.

Since the early 1970s, the Jaime Herrera-Navarres organization has run a major heroin smuggling operation between Mexico and the United States. The Herrera organization is now estimated to have 3,000 to 5,000 members, many of whom are either naturalized American citizens or illegal aliens residing in this country.[14]

Mexican heroin production declined in the late 1970s due to eradication programs, poor weather conditions, and better enforcement. At the same time, heroin production in Southeast Asia accelerated dramatically. By 1976, the "Golden Triangle" of Burma, Thailand, and Laos was supplying the United States with increasing amounts of heroin.

Chinese organized-crime groups, known as triads, or secret societies, have taken over that part of the heroin distribution in the United States that was formerly dominated by La Cosa Nostra. As a result, the "Chinese Connection," has increased the Golden Triangle's share from 14 percent in 1985 to nearly 20 percent in 1986.[15]

Triads have existed in the United States since the 1840s, when large numbers of Chinese immigrants arrived. The triads have "business relationships" with some Chinese gangs, or tongs, in the United States. But although a tong may or may not be engaged in illegal activities, a triad is by nature a criminal organization. Today, many fear a rash of triad crime in the United States due to the recent emigration of many triad members to this country.

Law-enforcement officials claim that Chinese criminals have become the dominant force in New York City's multibillion-dollar heroin industry. They are involved in extortion, prostitution, loan sharking, gun smuggling, and murder. From New York City, their operations are spreading to Boston, Philadelphia, Houston, Dallas, Portland, and other cities.

Officials fear that Chinese organized crime could eventually achieve as much influence as the Mafia. According to some sources, the effect of Chinese heroin distribution is being felt in black and Hispanic neighborhoods where the Chinese crime group is supplying heroin that is three to ten times more potent than usual.

The Golden Triangle produces 60 tons of heroin every year. Khun Sa is the warlord who controls the flow of heroin. He operates according to a set of rigid, life-or-death rules. Khun Sa reportedly buried alive a Thai government informant suspected of leading soldiers to his headquarters. He hanged another. Sa offered bounties for any Americans killed in the Golden Triangle, which he regards as his own territory. The wife of U.S. drug-enforcement agent Michael Powers was shot dead on the main street of the Thai town of Chiang Mai.[16]

The DEA believes that Khun Sa controls 80 percent of the 90 or more tons of heroin that will be produced this year from Golden Triangle opium. His 15,000 well-equipped, highly disciplined, and well-armed men protect his drug domain brutally and effectively. In 1982, the Thai army launched an attack against Khun Sa. In the battle that followed, seventeen soldiers and eighty of Sa's men were killed and a village was completely destroyed. But Sa continued in the heroin trade.[17]

Heroin from Southeast Asia most frequently arrives in the United States in small amounts. Mostly, the drug is smuggled in by passengers traveling on commercial airlines, or concealed in legitimate shipments of air and sea cargo, such as textiles or sports equipment.

Since 1979, another major source of heroin in the United States has been the Golden Crescent. This is an area of Southwest Asia that includes parts of Pakistan, Afghanistan, and Iran. Golden Crescent heroin is trafficked into the United States by a variety of narcotics organizations in Pakistan, Lebanon, India, and West Africa. By the time the drug arrives here it has undergone a geometric rise in price. Around $12,500 worth of the raw material when converted to heroin is worth $1.7 million in street sales![18]

MARIJUANA

From the 1930s through the mid-1970s, Mexican drug traffickers supplied nearly all of the marijuana consumed in the United States. The Mexican monopoly ended in 1975 when authorities sprayed Paraquat, a potent herbicide that is toxic to humans, on the Mexican crop and destroyed much of it.

During the mid-1970s, Colombian criminal groups stepped in to fill the vacuum left by the lack of Mexican marijuana. Since then, the Colombians have used a special approach. They oversee the cultivation and export of marijuana. Then, in an arrangement known as off-loading, they hire "service providers" to ship the drug. The off-loaders never actually own the marijuana; they just collect a fee for its safe transfer. Once in the United States, the drug is delivered to a distributor, who in turn supplies lower-level dealers.

The marijuana plant, *Cannabis sativa*, also known as hemp, grows under a wide range of conditions. Once harvested, the plant requires no refining and very little processing. The leaves and flowers contain the psychoactive ingredient, THC (tetrahydrocannabinol).

Mexico and Colombia each produce about 30 percent of the American marijuana supply. Southeast Asia also harvests a considerable amount, but far less of this marijuana reaches here. Its large bulk and strong aroma make it expensive and risky to transport. Thus, domestic cultivators have stepped in; about one-fourth of the marijuana used in the United States is grown here.

Smaller groups are also able to enter the drug market because of marijuana's comparatively low wholesale cost. But marijuana sales generate a small profit in comparison to other illicit drugs. The reason is that marijuana, unlike heroin or cocaine, is not diluted, or "cut," during the intermediate phases of trafficking. It is sold in much the same form at the wholesale and retail levels. And it changes hands as few as two or three times from the grower to the user.

Since the early 1980s, domestic growers have adopted innovative farming techniques, such as indoor cultivation and hydroponics, to increase marijuana production. They can also turn out a stronger drug at a lower price, a factor that gives American growers a considerable advantage over foreign competitors.

Only large criminal organizations have the resources and connections necessary to generate large profits from marijuana trafficking. Many groups that deal in other drugs, such as heroin and cocaine, can and do facilitate the movement of marijuana to the United States.

TRAFFICKING IN OTHER DRUGS

Millions of Americans abuse a number of licit and illicit drugs other than heroin, cocaine, and marijuana. These include tranquilizers, stimulants, synthetic, or designer, drugs, hallucinogens, and depressants. Most popular among these dangerous drugs are diazepam (Valium), amphetamine ("speed"), and PCP.

Dangerous drugs are available to the consumer from secret laboratories in the United States and other sources. Many of the drugs are approved for medical use in the United States and reach the illicit market through underground networks. A significant portion of the U.S. supply of certain drugs, notably the amphetamines and diazepam, is diverted from legal channels in foreign countries and smuggled into the United States. The amphetamines, for example, often come across the border from Canada.[19]

Certain parts of the traffic in dangerous drugs show organized-crime involvement. But the sales of amphetamines and PCP appear to be dominated nationwide by outlaw motorcycle gangs. According to a survey of local law-enforcement officials, these gangs have long been active in trafficking a variety of illicit drugs. Today they control nearly 40 percent of the illegal drug traffic in the United States.

The gangs have found ways to manufacture amphetamines and PCP and thus have gained control over the distribution of these two drugs. Officials estimate that nearly all the U.S. traffic in PCP is run by motorcycle gangs. According to the DEA, the gangs "are believed to control the entire amphetamine market."[20]

Of the estimated 3,500 motorcycle gangs in the United States, about 1,000 are involved in drug trafficking. They operate in every state of the nation. In 1983, a biker named Clarence "Addie" Crouch told a congressional committee about the initiation ceremony. "When a new member joins, he has six months to roll his bones—to kill someone. If they don't roll bones, they are killed," he said.[21]

The major outlaw motorcycle gangs traffic drugs in separate territories: Hell's Angels control the West Coast; the Outlaws dominate the Midwest and parts of the East Coast; the Bandidos control the Southwest; and the eastern seaboard states are dominated by the Pagans.

Hell's Angels, the oldest of the four motorcycle gangs, first become involved in drug distribution in the late 1960s. Initially, the group trafficked marijuana, heroin, cocaine, seconal, PCP, and amphetamines. In the 1970s, amphetamine production increased, and within a short period of time the Hell's Angels organization dominated West Coast amphetamine manufacture and distribution. Since 1970, police have recorded thirty-six murders committed by the Angels' northern California chapter alone. "The majority of the murder and violence is centered around narcotics and drugs," one police official said.[22]

In the eastern United States, the Pagans' gang leadership recruited chemists and gained control of the amphetamine and PCP markets from Florida to New England. The Pagans' drug activity became centered in the

Philadelphia/south New Jersey area. Although the Pagans were once rivals of the Bruno organized-crime family, they now cooperate, especially in amphetamine and PCP manufacture and distribution. Officials believe that the Bruno leadership finances part of the Pagans' drug activities in return for some of the profits and protection.

Among motorcycle gangs, skirmishes over territory have turned into wars for the control of drug distribution. On occasion these wars have been fought with .50-caliber machine guns mounted on trucks called "war wagons." Two former bikers recently testified before a congressional committee investigating motorcycle gangs. Edward Jackson said, "Right now the Pagans are larger than the organized-crime families. They are engaged in the ruthless aspect of organized crime that was common in the 1920s and 1930s."[23]

The involvement of organized crime in trafficking dangerous drugs other than the amphetamines and PCP in the United States is not well known. But everyone is aware of the enormous profits that can be made from the synthetic, laboratory-made designer drugs, and their relative ease of manufacture. Since making and selling designer drugs seems to be an activity perfectly suited to organized-crime groups, experts assume they already control this part of the drug market.

Drug gangs are active within many prisons in the United States. In California the trafficking business within correctional institutions is believed to be worth about $1 million a year. Gangs such as Nuestra Familia ("Our Family"), the Mexican Mafia, the Aryan Brotherhood, and the Black Guerrilla family are well represented. They supply LSD and pills to prisoners—"anything that's wanted, they've got," according to one law-enforcement official.[24] Murders, stabbings, and beatings are a common part of the prison drug trade. One prison official expressed a widespread concern: "We are forever fearful that one of those murdered is going to be one of us."[25]

CONCLUSION

Today's longtime, powerful Mafia groups are largely in disarray. A crackdown by the FBI and federal prosecutors has led to long prison terms for old bosses of organized-crime families along with many of their top lieutenants. Although still involved in narcotics trafficking, most of the families are less powerful than they once were.

New mobsters have moved into their places. Many of them are even more violent and ruthless than the traditional Mafia families. The new mobsters for the most part have different values than their elders. They are more interested in making money quickly and more willing to engage in large-scale drug trafficking.

Young Mafia members and so-called mob yuppies—groups of Colombians, Asians, and motorcycle gangs—are said to be reshaping organized crime. The number of members and the amount of monies they have accumulated far exceed anything in the history of organized crime.

Violence in the underworld of top-level drug trafficking is different from the violence on the level of dealers and individual drug users. The elimination of drug-trafficking and the violence associated with organized crime have to do with the much larger issue of law enforcement and public policy. A decided shift in both areas may be the only answer to the problem of drug-trafficking and organized-crime violence.

CHAPTER

LAW ENFORCEMENT
AND VIOLENCE

■ *A twenty-six-year-old undercover police officer was killed in a routine "buy-and-bust" operation. While an arrest team waited outside the building, one of the drug dealers escaped.*

■ *Seven police officers, acting on a tip that 2 kilograms (4.4 lb) of cocaine were in an apartment, broke the door down. The woman inside bolted into her bedroom, slamming the door behind her. When a police officer followed her, she fired through the closed door, killing him.*

■ *Two former Miami policemen were found guilty of raiding a cocaine-laden boat with the intention of stealing the drug for themselves. Three traffickers, trying to escape what they thought was a genuine police raid, jumped into the river and drowned.*

■ *The police recently began a foot patrol in an Omaha, Nebraska, housing project where two rival Los Angeles gangs frequently clash, and gunfire and violence erupt. Residents say the drug dealers have merely moved their operation beyond the view of the patrols.*

A social contract exists in this country that authorizes the police to capture and arrest, and, if absolutely necessary, to injure or kill individuals who would cause such harm to others. But in their efforts to stop violence, the police are often harmed themselves. At times, they feel compelled to use excessive force and unnecessary violence themselves.

Traditionally, people have respected law-enforcement officers. But things seem to be changing. Said New York City's mayor Edward Koch, "Now they [criminals] go out of their way to kill cops."[1]

How can the police most effectively combat drugs and drug-related violence in our society? How can we reduce the risk of violence against police? And how can we prevent the police from exceeding their authority in enforcing the law against suspected drug dealers and others in the drug trade?

POLICE
AGAINST VIOLENCE

In Los Angeles County, the cops made more than 12,000 gang-related arrests in an attempt to disrupt the activities of an estimated 70,000 drug-gang members.[2] Many other police departments in small and big cities have scored similar successes in convicting drug dealers. But despite their best efforts, drug trafficking flourishes on a major scale. And the biggest crime problem this nation has seen in many decades continues unabated.

Local police do the best they can to curb the drug trade and the violence that it spawns. They disrupt low-level dealing with periodic street sweeps. But the dealers merely regroup and set up shop somewhere else. Sterling Johnson, special narcotics prosecutor for New York State, likens it to "turning off a faucet." But in this case, the faucet won't shut off.[3]

Detectives and special agents within police departments go after the drug kingpins. Arrests of important traffickers interrupt the flow of drugs into communities and force the high-level dealers and distributors to change their method of operation. But these major figures often continue to run their businesses from jail even as rivals fight over their territory.

Law-enforcement officials often solve crimes with information they get from victims and from witnesses. In many drug-related crimes, however, people are reluctant to talk, for several reasons. Perhaps strongest is the fear of reprisal—against themselves or members of their family—for going to the police. Another reason is that victims of drug-related offenses are often addicts or dealers, people who are already on the wrong side of the law. And finally, "ratting" on anyone within the drug community is considered highly unacceptable behavior, often subject to harsh punishment by dealers or others.

The reluctance of witnesses to talk, the unpredictable nature of crimes among drug distributors, dealers, and users, and the usual absence of evidence make it extremely difficult for the police to catch the offenders. To achieve any sort of success in catching drug criminals—and even more important, to prevent drug-related crimes from occurring—the police must turn to informants and undercover intelligence systems that operate within the gangs and drug organizations.

Informants are often persons who are themselves involved in the drug trade and other criminal activities. The informant is often given a kind of license to continue his or her life with drugs as a reward for helping law-enforcement agents. The chief narcotics officer in Baltimore once claimed that there were 800 active narcotics informers, who had committed crimes, working with the police. Most of these informers were actually dealers. The police allowed them to operate freely as long as they helped the police arrest and convict others in the drug trade.[4]

The contact between law-enforcement agents and criminals in the drug community who serve as undercover operators or informants is potentially corrupting. The huge amounts of money involved and the temptations of the drugs themselves often make it a small step from using informants to doing business with them.

Drug-related crimes of violence, especially those involving murder or serious injury, are on the rise. The increase is due, in part, to the proliferation of high-powered weapons in the hands of the drug criminals. The police in the front lines of the war against the drug criminals are suffering heavy losses from these weapons. Many law-enforcement officials now are winning the right to increase their own supply of more advanced, more powerful guns.

Police Chief Maurice Turner, Jr., of Washington, D.C., wants his officers to be as well armed as the drug dealers they are facing. He proposes outfitting cops in squad cars with shotguns and arming every officer with a 9-mm semiautomatic weapon.[5] On the federal level, the Drug Enforcement Administration is issuing 9-mm submachine guns to its agents as replacement for their revolvers and semiautomatic pistols.[6]

Increasing police firepower has revived the so-called deadly force dilemma: when should police shoot and when should they hold their fire? Officers who shoot run the risk of executing a suspect without a trial or injuring or killing bystanders. Both of these outcomes are morally wrong and lead to public outrage and condemnation in the press. Officers who decide not to shoot risk losing their own lives and those of their partners. Unwittingly, they may also allow a guilty person to escape. Unfortunately, the important decision must be made in a split second under the most intense pressure!

To control violence in the streets, police departments frequently send patrols to high-crime streets or neighborhoods. The theory is that a visible police presence in the street will deter crime. But this tactic, some say, is of limited value. Part of the problem is that many violent crimes, such as murder and aggravated assault, occur out of the sight of the police. And even when the police are on the scene, these crimes flare up so quickly that the police usually have no chance to intervene.

Law-enforcement agencies have a couple of special tactics that they use in their attempt to control drug-related crime. One approach is to use a decoy. A police officer who dresses and acts like a potential victim is sent into a drug-infested, high-crime area. As soon as he or she is attacked, the officer makes the arrest, backed up by other officers who are waiting in hiding. Police officers, hidden in cars, trucks, or buildings, will also sometimes "stake out," or keep watch, on locations where crimes are particularly likely to occur.

The "jumpout" is a favorite strategy of Washington, D.C.'s twenty-five-man Narcotics Task Force—a group that made 2,700 arrests in 1987.[7] A team of undercover cops cruises around some of the seventy known open-air drug markets in an unmarked car. When they spot someone who looks like a dealer, one of the officers approaches, makes the purchase, and pays with marked money. The officer then returns to the car and radios in a description of the dealer. Other officers move in quickly for the arrest.

Police say jumpouts lead to arrests 90 percent of the time. But they admit that some dealers are wise to their methods. Lookouts are trained to warn dealers about possible police jumpouts. In one case, the suspect actually swallowed the drugs that the police needed for evidence as he was about to be nabbed!

A new weapon against drug gangs is the federal Racketeer Influenced and Corrupt Organizations Act (RICO). It can be used to convict gang members for "engaging in a pattern of criminal activity"; the maximum sentence is twenty-five years. Sometimes RICO can put drug dealers behind bars, even if they cannot be convicted of murder, assault, or other violent crimes.

For most police officers, the danger of being killed or permanently disabled on the job is very real. Nearly a hundred police are killed in the United States each year, 90 percent of them by guns, which are often in the hands of people involved with drugs.[8]

Rampant gang-related violence in our cities seems to be undermining the average citizen's confidence in the criminal-justice system. Many murders, including those of cops, are designed to be intimidating. Not only do they frighten individual witnesses, but they also spread fear throughout the city, including among judges and the courts.

Many believe that the gangs will grow bigger and consolidate their hold on drug trafficking. With growth will come even greater skill in evading law enforcement. The supply and demand for drugs seem almost limitless. Without a coordinated national strategy for combating the spread of drugs, American cops are hard pressed to put up an effective fight.

POLICE USE
OF VIOLENCE

Experts warn that rampant drug trafficking and extraordinary police efforts to control it threaten the integrity of law-enforcement agencies. In late 1988, six New York City police officers or former officers were charged with various crimes: robbing drug dealers in the Bronx, holding up a grocery store in Brooklyn, and robbing an undercover officer who was posing as a drug dealer. Several former Miami policemen stole money and cocaine, which they later sold, from people they arrested in the Miami streets and from boats in the Miami River.[9] In these cases drug abuse by the officers is suspected to have been the motive.

A thirty-year-old New Jersey police officer indulged his $500-a-day cocaine habit while on patrol in his car. As his addiction grew, he paid for the drugs by extorting protection money and drugs from the dealers and criminals he was sworn to arrest.[10]

Three police officers suspected of drug abuse demanded $6,000 from a restaurant owner. They threatened to arrest his daughter-in-law on a narcotics charge and to have her two children sent to a foster home unless he paid them. The restaurant owner paid them what they asked.[11]

Police officers in Miami and some other cities in Dade County, Florida, have been accused of not always arresting the drug traffickers they captured. Instead, they stole the traffickers' cocaine and in a few cases killed them as well.[12]

The police are especially vulnerable to drug abuse for two reasons: drugs are widely used and even accepted in the United States, and many officers come from communities where the people around them are on drugs. "Today you have a generation of police officers who grew up where drugs were common," said Thomas A. Reppetto of the Citizen's Crime Commission. "Now they're set down in neighborhoods where drugs are being used and sold—a certain number of people are eventually going to succumb."[13]

In recent years, many older police officers have been replaced by young recruits, causing the average age of the officers to drop lower and lower. Today's rookies, experts say, are not only younger, they are better educated and more liberal than the police of the past. More tolerant of different lifestyles, they may not condemn drug abuse as strenuously as cops of the older generation.

Most people assume that the fear of arrest deters the criminal. But the present drug crisis has jammed the courts and crowded the prisons. All but the most serious drug offenders are released and are back on the streets very soon. Frequently, the only punishment for being arrested on a drug charge is an arrest record. This so-called revolving door of justice frustrates many law-enforcement officials interested in winning the war against illegal drugs.

Like anyone who constantly works against great odds, a police officer may eventually become discouraged and even dishonest. This is what happens to some narcotics cops. They stop caring, turn cynical, and sometimes just walk away from problems. Or they may become so passionate and determined to end the drug scourge that they resort to illegal—even violent—means to enforce the law as they see it.

Although the number of shootings of police by civilians, and civilians by police has been going down since 1974, the figures are still very high.[14] Statistics show that civilians are ten times more likely to be killed by police than vice versa. People who believe that the police misuse their force and power tend to be resentful and hostile. Such individuals create situations that can erupt into riots and mass violence in the street.

Almost everyone agrees that getting rid of drugs is a worthy goal, for our nation and for the many people, young and old, whose lives are being destroyed by drugs. But are police ever justified in committing a wrong to achieve a worthy end? The "wrong" alternatives include using violent methods—beatings and physical and psychological torture—to get information or a confession. Some police assume that anything goes, as long as the purpose is to cut down on the drug trade.

Of course, properly trained police do not usually use illegal means to enforce the law. And police who resort to "dirty" tactics are very often caught and punished.

ANTIDRUG RAGE AND LAWLESSNESS IN THE COMMUNITY

The violent crimes connected with the widespread use of crack and other drugs have left citizens asking for better police protection. They demand that greater efforts be made to catch and prosecute those committing the crimes. All too often, these citizens feel either that their cries for help are being ignored or that officials are incapable of stemming the rising tide of violence.

This sets a vicious circle into motion. Crime victims do not call the police because they feel that they will not get any help. The criminals, feeling safe from capture by the police, escalate the frequency and intensity of their attacks.

Desperate to regain control of their communities, honest individuals sometimes decide to take steps to protect themselves and to clean up their drug-infested neighborhoods. In several instances this has led to citizens taking the law into their own hands.

In Miami, citizens committed six acts of arson against crack houses, including a fire that destroyed three houses on March 17, 1988. In Detroit, two men set fire to a crack house. On Long Island, a fifty-seven-year-old man opened fire with a 12-gauge shotgun on a crowd of people believed to be dealing drugs near his home. The man said he feared the effects that drug dealing on his street was having on his grandchildren. A crowd in New York City attacked and killed a man known as a drug addict after he was seen robbing a woman who had only $10 on her.

Certain neighborhoods have formed patrols made up of residents in the community. Their activism grows out of a sense of despair and a loss of faith in law enforcement. Richard Behar, a member of one citizens' patrol, told of his decision to organize the patrol: "You feel violence in your heart and for the first time in my life I actually wanted to kill people. It was a horrible feeling. And I knew that if I was feeling it, others were feeling it."[15]

In April 1988, tenants of a Washington, D.C., housing project invited members of the Nation of Islam to patrol their buildings in an effort to drive out the crack and cocaine dealers. The patrol group, with its reputation for "disciplined, relentless toughness," patrolled the project on foot and in vans. Ten Muslims kicked and stomped a man who, they said, had pulled a shotgun on them.

In a similar situation in Roosevelt, New York, Muslims aided police in arresting a drug dealer. In describing the violent methods they used, Detective Sergeant Richards Hayes said, "They beat him [the dealer] up. The guy is in the hospital."[16]

Police officials have warned that vigilantism—unauthorized acts of citizens aimed at maintaining order and punishing the criminals by themselves—could provoke further violence. They have urged groups of individuals not to take violent actions against drug dealers. Instead, they have encouraged citizens' groups to find ways to work hand in hand with the police.

One of the most successful outcomes of police and community interaction occurred in Lynn, Massachusetts. Here, drug dealers operated openly in areas a few blocks from the downtown business district. Runners freely hawked their wares to pedestrians and drivers passing by. And drug users from all over the state came to Lynn to buy heroin and other high-potency drugs.

In September 1983, the county organized a Drug Task Force to crack down on drugs in the community. Its object was to stop heroin buyers and sellers from coming to Lynn. It was hoped this would lead to a reduction of drug sales and crime.

In the first ten months, 186 arrests were made. Ninety-six defendants were convicted or pleaded guilty. The effect on crime was noticeable. Within a year, robberies dropped 18.5 percent and burglaries were down 37.5 percent. Despite a reduction in drug-enforcement staff, burglaries remained at their lower level in 1985 and robberies declined still further.

Researchers are still trying to decide why the Lynn results were so good and why similar efforts in Lawrence, Massachusetts, and elsewhere have met with failure. What they have learned is the following:

■ *The enforcement effort should be proportionate to the size of the opposing trafficking networks.*

■ *The police should carry out the operations after obtaining widespread community support.*

■ *The police should maintain the greatest respect for the laws governing search and seizure.*

■ *And finally, street-level enforcement should go along with treatment for offenders. Otherwise, the benefits of drug enforcement will not be fully realized.*[17]

CONCLUSION

United States law enforcement against the drug trade presently involves two types of effort, one for street dealers and users, the other for mid- and high-level dealers. Each effort produces different difficulties and different effects on the drug trade.

Police officers involved with street-level enforcement—patrols, jumpouts, street sweeps, arrests and seizures—temporarily interrupt the supply of drugs on the local level. Disruption at the point of purchase usually means fewer customers for street dealers and reduced robberies and burglaries. But these policies also have a down side. Shortages may create higher prices. The higher prices may lead users to commit more crimes, just to pay the high costs of the drug. And the higher number of arrests overburdens law-enforcement efforts and the criminal-justice system.

Where police departments have separate vice or narcotics units, detectives devote their time to catching the kingpins of the drug trade. Vigorous prosecution of high-level dealers forces some to quit, or to at least cut back their operations. But these actions, too, act to drive up the price and increase the attempts of new groups to gain control of areas vacated by the kingpins. Often, the police and prosecutors become overwhelmed by the number of drug cases and frustrated that drug dealers spend so little time behind bars because of overcrowded prisons.

Law enforcement has the potential for unlawful violence against offenders. Although it remains one of the most effective means of controlling the drug crisis, public policies against drugs and crime need to be considered.

CHAPTER

7

POLICY MAKING
AND VIOLENCE

■ *Less than two weeks after police left a Chicago neighborhood where they had arrested large numbers of small dealers and buyers, crack dealers and their customers reappeared in even greater numbers.*

■ *For nineteen months, New York City paid a private armed security service to guard a city-owned apartment building to control drug traffic and crime. Despite the program and its very high cost, drug problems in and around the building continued.*

■ *In Houston, a hub for border drug traffic, police connected eight drug assassinations to the Colombians in 1988. Law-enforcement officials began bracing for a full-scale drug war.*

■ *Recently, a team of American drug agents dropped in on an estate in Roma, Texas, on the border of the United States and Mexico. The agents broke up a network that they said had put 3,000 pounds (1,360 kg) of marijuana a week onto American streets.*

■ *The eradication of nearly 3,000 acres (1,200 hectares) of Bolivian coca plants wiped out only 3 percent of the country's total crop. At the same time it stimulated even more planting in different areas.*

Many different approaches for dealing with drug trafficking have been tried in the United States. None has proved very successful. We must now set priorities, since the resources available for fighting the drug menace are extremely limited.

Shall we increase the penalties for drug-related crimes or decriminalize drugs altogether?

Shall we work to stop the supply of drugs or go after the users?

Shall we continue to support foreign governments that are friendly to the United States even though they are drug-producing and exporting countries?

Experts debate the relative value of the various strategies. But everyone agrees something must be done. In a *New York Times*/CBS News poll taken in March 1988, respondents were asked which of five leading international issues was the most important facing this country. The largest proportion, 48 percent, cited drug trafficking.[1]

What are the main strategies being considered?

LEGALIZATION OF DRUGS

Making heroin and cocaine legal is an approach to eliminating drug trafficking that is always brought up but rarely taken very seriously. Strictly speaking, legalization can mean lifting all restrictions on the production, distribution, possession, or use of any drug. Or, it may mean bringing drug trafficking under effective control by allowing limited use of certain drugs, producing the drugs under government auspices, distributing them through tightly regulated distribution systems, and punishing severely any production or use outside the authorized system.

Supporters of legalization suggest that such a move would undercut the mob's profit and eliminate the role of organized crime in drug trafficking. Legitimate business people would enter the business. There would be less violence, since the industry would have access to the police to solve crimes and to the courts to settle disputes.

And instead of draining away tax dollars in expensive enforcement efforts, the drug sellers would help the economy by paying taxes.

Drug use under legalization might be less destructive to users and to society. Compared to present policy, the drugs people use would be less expensive, purer, and easier to obtain.

Opponents to legalization argue that making drugs more available would significantly increase the number of drug users. This rise in use would impose a huge health cost on the nation, thus undercutting the gains from reducing crime. To take only two examples, drug-taking spreads AIDS through shared needles; also, a high proportion of children born to cocaine users suffer from brain abnormalities. The health risks, plus the idea that drug use is immoral are two among many arguments against outright legalization.

What about a halfway measure—one that keeps in place most of the restrictions on drugs but still leaves room for the legitimate use of some drugs? Wouldn't such a policy give some of the benefits of legalization without increasing the levels of drug use?

Those who oppose such legislation claim that black markets will develop outside any boundaries that are drawn between legitimate and illicit use of drugs. Indeed, some say, the more limited the boundary, the larger and more controlling will be the role of organized crime in black-market operations.

Under today's drug laws, barbiturates, amphetamines, and tranquilizers may be used for a variety of medical purposes; they are, however, obtainable only with a physician's prescription through a licensed pharmacy. Cocaine is presently legal for use as a local anesthetic by dentists. Although heroin and marijuana are illegal, some research uses of these drugs are permitted, and they are currently being considered for certain medical applications, such as in the treatment of terminally ill cancer patients.

The comparatively few legal uses of illicit drugs have had little effect on criminal trafficking. Some portion of the demand for amphetamines, barbiturates, and tranquilizers is met by diverting drugs from legitimate channels. But the current demand for such drugs as marijuana, heroin, and cocaine makes virtually the entire distribution system illicit and dependent on drug trafficking.

ERADICATION
OF ILLICIT CROPS

The policy of eliminating the raw materials used to produce the drugs is another proposed way to deal with drug trafficking. For heroin, cocaine, and marijuana, this means controlling opium, coca leaf, and marijuana crops in countries such as Turkey, Afghanistan, Thailand, Bolivia, Colombia, Peru, Mexico, and Jamaica. For marijuana, the control of production within the United States is also important.

Efforts to check the illicit drug crops generally take one of two forms. The government tries to induce farmers to stop growing the crops. Or the government attempts to destroy the crops. In some instances the inducement is a payment of money to the farmer for not cultivating the drug plants or rural development so other crops can be grown and harvested. To destroy the crops the government either sprays, digs up, or burns the farmers' fields.

Eradication of drug-producing plants through airborne chemical spraying, advocates claim, requires few workers and destroys the drugs right at the source. Opponents point out that the chemicals may also have potentially harmful health effects on farmers and their families and may do a great deal of unintentional damage to legitimate crops. An American diplomat was recently in the embarrassing position of advocating aerial eradication of foreign drug crops at the same time as American courts were ruling against spraying American-grown marijuana with the same chemicals.[2]

Ground-level destruction by digging up the plants has other problems. Among the biggest disadvantages is this one: large numbers of workers are necessary, and with so many people involved, there can be no element of surprise. The farmer will know of their coming well in advance of the operations.

All eradication efforts face two major difficulties. First, there is no shortage of locations where the crops may be grown. If Turkey stops growing opium poppies, Mexico, Afghanistan, and Southeast Asia can take up the slack. If Bolivia stops growing coca, Peru can step in. If Mexico eliminates marijuana production, the hills of California would be even more densely filled with marijuana plants than at present.

Also, foreign governments cannot always be relied on to enforce crop-control policies. In some cases the crops are very important to the domestic economy or the personal well-being of high government officials. Often the farmers are so strong a political bloc that the government prefers not to act at all.

In Bolivia, for example, many of the 100,000 peasants growing coca are members of powerful unions and cooperatives. "If you tried to spray," one U.S. State Department official said, "you'd start a revolution."[3]

Sometimes the problem with crop eradication involves inefficiency or corruption in the agencies that are supposed to be carrying out the programs. Other times the crops are grown in parts of the country that are not under effective governmental control.

Corruption is widespread among political and military leaders, the police, and the judiciary in virtually every country touched by the drug trade. Enormous amounts of money are generated through drug transactions, and there is always the threat of harm to enemies of the drug traffickers. This combination of factors makes it just too tempting for many in positions of authority to resist corruption.

Officials, from the lowly town constable to those in top elected positions, are bribed regularly by the drug traffickers. These corrupt officials then work to protect the interest of the drug growers, processors, and smugglers. Allegations of such corruption continually surface in Mexico, the largest single source of heroin and marijuana flowing into the United States.

In March 1985, after DEA agent Enrique ("Kiki") Camarena and his pilot, Alfredo Zavala Avelar, were kidnapped and murdered, six Mexican police officers were indicted on charges of assisting the drug traffickers.[4] Official corruption in Mexico significantly undermines cooperation with the United States, according to the State Department's annual drug report.[5]

What happens when the government of a country that is a major drug source cannot, or will not, cooperate with the United States's antidrug efforts? The U.S. government must then balance its drug-policy objectives against its foreign-policy objectives. Usually this means doing nothing at all.

Governments such as those in Panama and Afghanistan pose this kind of problem to the United States. They are important to the United States as bulwarks against communist expansion. Yet they are also major centers of drug trafficking. Often our government feels forced to overlook drug trafficking in order to encourage those governments' anticommunist activities.

The Panama case, involving that country's leader, General Manuel Antonio Noriega, is one of several instances where our drug problems have clashed with our political needs. Apparently General Noriega's political value to the United States has outweighed the concerns about his heavy involvement with drug traffickers.

The poppy cultivation in Afghanistan is another case in point. The crop there is currently at record high levels.

Much of it grows in areas controlled by anticommunist guerrillas. American administration officials, who support the guerrillas, never raise the drug issue with them. "We're not going to let a little thing like drugs get in the way of the political situation," is how one official put it.[6]

Drug-trafficking organizations in many areas of the world are allied with terrorists. Their typical relationship is mutually beneficial: the traffickers supply the terrorists with American currency and weapons in return for protection and assistance in their drug-smuggling activities. Terrorists funded through drug trafficking could possibly become powerful enough to disrupt a number of countries presently allied with the United States and thus threaten this country's national security.

One such group currently operating in Peru is the Maoist Shining Path (Sendero Luminoso). This group seeks a rural-based revolution to rid the country of the "imperialistic" influence of the United States and other foreign governments. They have incited peasants, many of whom make their living from coca cultivation, to rebel against anticoca projects in major growing areas. Not long ago, several anticoca projects were attacked by armed mobs, resulting in many injuries and deaths.

Colombia offers another example of how drug traffickers can block eradication efforts. Peasants believed to be acting on orders of traffickers complained to health authorities of illness after a relatively harmless herbicide was sprayed on some marijuana crops. The complaints put an end to the eradication project.

A 1987 series of violent attacks by traffickers on police units and eradication workers in Peru led to the torture and murder of nineteen members of an American-financed coca-eradication team. This attack was followed by the brutal murder of seventeen American-backed eradicators by about fifty traffickers armed with submachine guns.[7] After these killings, eradication in those areas controlled by terrorists and drug traffickers plummeted.

Tough American talk on fighting drugs overseas has not been matched by tough diplomatic action. In 1986, for example, Congress passed an antidrug law imposing economic sanctions against countries that do not cooperate fully with American efforts to reduce the drug trade. Those that do not comply are to suffer economic penalties.[8]

But the law has never been used to penalize a nation considered an ally, such as Afghanistan, Turkey, Panama, Paraguay, Laos, and many others. In Laos, as an example, the United States is said to believe that any censure could jeopardize negotiations for the return of the remains of American servicemen killed during the Vietnam War.

The military branch of our government consistently opposes the idea of playing any role in the drug war. Some top officers are unwilling to participate because of fears that the drug effort would take money away from other programs more central to the military's mission. Others fear that any American military action against drug traffickers might lure American service personnel into drug use or the drug trade.

History, though, has shown that some eradication policies can work. In the early 1970s the Turkish government was able to establish control over the cultivation of opium poppies in that country. This resulted in a major reduction in the supply of heroin to the United States East Coast for two or three years. The drop in supply resulted in an observable reduction in the rate at which new people were becoming addicted. A similar policy in Mexico also affected supply and demand for both heroin and marijuana in the 1970s.

But most eradication programs are not long-term solutions; they are unpredictable at best. Perhaps the United States should exploit opportunities in foreign countries when they arise but not depend on eradication as its main approach to drug control.

INTERDICTION

Interdiction aims at stopping illicit drugs at the border; it is considered an important way to stop the drug trade. With interdiction, rather than depending on foreign governments for help in solving our drug problem, we attempt to solve it by ourselves.

Several government agencies have special powers to conduct searches for illicit drugs along the coasts and borders. Members of the U.S. Customs Agency and Immigration and Naturalization Service inspect people and goods passing through official points of entry. And the Coast Guard, the military, and civilian aviation authorities all may check goods and people entering the country.

The main problem with interdiction is the size of the task. United States borders are more than 12,000 miles (19,300 km) long. Our border with Mexico alone is 2,000 miles (3,200 km). Federal agencies cannot possibly hope to guard that entire length. The fact is that only an estimated 10 percent of illicit drugs are stopped at the border.[9]

Meanwhile, drug traffickers have so much money that they can afford to lay out millions for ships, planes, trucks, couriers, and bribes. They use all these resources to avoid and outwit the authorities.

Another problem is the sheer quantity of material that comes into our country. Over 420 billion tons of goods cross the borders each year. In comparison, the quantities of illegal drugs are very small—just a few hundred tons of marijuana and less than 20 tons of heroin or cocaine. Although the harm they cause is considerable, the drugs are only a tiny bit of our annual imports.[10]

The fact that interdiction operations are divided among many agencies presents other difficulties. Some of these government forces have had severe budget cuts in recent years. The Coast Guard, for example, whose mission is to intercept drugs coming into the country by sea, conducted 55 percent fewer patrols in 1988 because Congress cut its budget by $100 million.[11]

Some of the best interdiction successes have been achieved with marijuana. Because it is so bulky and has a distinctive odor, marijuana is relatively easy to detect. This does not help the drug situation very much, many say, because marijuana presents fewer problems than heroin or cocaine. Moreover, marijuana can be grown easily in the United States. If foreign supplies are kept out, the supply system can adjust by growing more marijuana domestically.

That seems to be exactly what has happened. Interdiction efforts are successful in seizing about a third of the marijuana destined for the United States. Yet, except for a few local areas, the impact on the price of availability of the drug has been minimal. American growers have more than made up for the shortfall. Worse, the current U.S.-grown marijuana is cheaper and more potent than the imported varieties.

HIGH-LEVEL
ENFORCEMENT
Drug agents nationwide focus many of their efforts on capturing and convicting the top traffickers. These are the people who are responsible for producing, importing, and distributing drugs. The basic aim is to paralyze or destroy the trafficking networks.

In the past, law-enforcement workers have called this approach "getting to Mr. Big." Experts believed that if the individual kingpin who controlled the drug-distribution network could be arrested, prosecuted, and imprisoned, the network would fall apart.

Today the law-enforcement community is becoming less and less certain that this strategy can succeed. Even when "Mr. Big" is in prison, they find, he can continue to manage his drug empire. Moreover, the nature of drug distribution seems to have changed. Organizations seem less dependent on single individuals. And the whole drug-distribution system is less centralized. Relatively small and fluid organizations now supply a large proportion of the illicit drugs.

Despite record confiscations of drugs in 1988 and a threefold increase in arrests of major drug traffickers, only a small percent of the cocaine and marijuana coming into the country has been seized. To deal with this problem, some police agents have shifted their strategy. Instead of going after individuals, they are trying to destroy whole networks. Federal investigators now have broad powers to seize all of the drug dealers' assets, including boats, cars, planes, houses, bank accounts, and cash.

This way of attacking illicit trafficking organizations is enormously expensive and time-consuming. Collecting enough evidence for a conviction usually requires informants, electronic surveillance, and infiltration into the drug organization by undercover agents. Then, at the trial, it is sometimes difficult to win a conviction. Complex laws protect the rights of the suspect, and the particular methods used to gather evidence may be considered illegal.

But even when it succeeds, the breakup of a drug-trafficking organization is not a complete victory. For every smashed drug ring with its leaders in jail there are others waiting to take over the territory and reap the huge profits to be made.

STREET-LEVEL ENFORCEMENT

Street-level enforcement depends mostly on the use of physical surveillance, the so-called buy-and-bust operations. While effective in the short run, this approach usually has little impact on the overall supply. Even though some dealers are arrested, they are quickly and easily replaced. At best, drug dealers may be driven off the street temporarily or forced to move to a different street.

A small task force committed to street-level drug enforcement, as took place in Lynn, Massachusetts, cut robberies by 18 percent and burglaries by 37 percent while it was in operation. However, an operation in Lawrence, Massachusetts, modeled after the Lynn program, failed to produce any important effect on levels of crime or drug use in that community.

To the extent that street-level enforcement increases the "hassle" associated with doing drugs, though, it achieves its objective of reducing drug use. When drugs, which are already expensive, are also made inconvenient to buy, some users may decide to abandon them. Those who are addicted are more tempted to go into a treatment program. And some of those who give up drugs are willing to cooperate with the police in breaking up the major trafficking networks. Ultimately, it can contribute to the quality of life in neighborhoods by returning the streets to community control.

CONCLUSION

If we are presently engaged in a "drug war," then the police are like the infantry—they clear the field. But breaking up drug rings and driving dealers from the streets is just the first step. There must also be national programs to ensure that the source of supply is permanently closed down. And there must be treatment and counseling programs, along with new initiatives in education, housing, and employment opportunities, to help remove the demand.

In the end, the real answer to the problem of drugs and violence is within our borders. The fight to win the war is up to all Americans. We need to get our priorities straight and back policies that put the fight against drug trafficking first and foremost. Then we must back up our policies with funds. The deadly connection between drugs and violence demands a sincere and determined national commitment to bring the problem under control.

SOURCE NOTES

CHAPTER 1

1. Peter Kerr, "Crime Study Finds Drug Use in Most Arrested," *The New York Times*, 22 January 1988, pp. A1, B4.
2. Robert M. Morgenthau, "Drug Habits We Can't Afford," *The New York Times*, 26 November 1988, p. 23.
3. James A. Inciardi, *The War on Drugs* (Palo Alto, Calif.: Mayfield, 1986), p. 140.
4. Evan Thomas, "The Enemy Within," *Time*, 15 September 1986, pp. 59–68.
5. Robert W. Amler, *Closing the Gap: The Burden of Unnecessary Illness* (New York: Oxford University Press, 1987), p. 89.
6. Jeffrey Fagan, Bruce Johnson, and Steven Belenko, *Crack and Changing Patterns of Drug Use, Abuse, and Criminality* (New York: Criminal Justice Agency, November 1987), p. 6.
7. David E. Pitt, "New York City, New Record for Slayings," *The New York Times*, 22 November 1988, p. B1.
8. Christopher A. Innes, *State Prison Inmate Survey: Drug Use and Crime* (Washington: National Institute of Justice, July 1988), p. 3.
9. Rita Kramer, *At a Tender Age: Violent Youth and Juvenile Justice* (New York: Holt and Co., 1988), p. 16.
10. Inciardi, p. 134.
11. Samuel G. Kling, *The Complete Guide to Everyday Law* (New York: Follet Publishing Co., 1973), pp. 487–500.

12. Innes, p. 5.
13. Inciardi, p. 135.
14. Kerr, p. B4.
15. Innes, p. 3.
16. Ibid., p. 6.
17. Bernard A. Gropper, *Probing the Links Between Drugs and Crime* (Washington: National Institute of Justice, February 1985), p. 4.
18. B. Drummond Ayres, "Washington Finds Drug War Is Hardest At Home," *The New York Times*, 9 December 1988, p. A22.
19. Phillip M. Boffey, "Drug Users, Not Suppliers Held Key Problem," *The New York Times*, 12 April 1988, pp. A1, A10.
20. Inciardi, p. 117.
21. Ibid., p. 118.
22. Boffey, p. A10.
23. "U.S. Crime Levels Show Rise," *The New York Times*, 10 September 1988, p. A11.
24. Ayres, p. A22.
25. Boffey, p. A10.

CHAPTER 2

1. Robert Cooke, "A Disease or Not," *Newsday*, 3 May 1988, Part III, p. 1.
2. Rachel V. *Family Secrets, Life Stories of Adult Children of Alcoholics* (New York: Harper & Row, 1987), p. xxxiv.
3. Alvin E. Bessent, "Boyfriend Accused of Slashing Woman," *Newsday*, 9 March 1988, p. 26.
4. Andrew H. Malcolm, "Drunken Driving: Zeroing In on the Hard Core," *The New York Times*, 12 May 1988, Sec. 4, p. 6.
5. Ibid.
6. Cooke, p. 1.
7. President's Commission on Organized Crime, *America's Habit, Drug Abuse, Drug Trafficking, and Organized Crime* (Washington: Government Printing Office, 1986), p. 33.
8. Phillip M. Boffey, "Drug Users, Not Suppliers Held Key Problem," *The New York Times*, 12 April 1988, p. A1.
9. Bernard A. Gropper, *Probing the Links Between Drugs and Crime*, (Washington: National Institute of Justice, February 1985), p. 3.
10. President's Commission, p. 38.
11. John S. Land with Ronald A. Taylor, "America on Drugs," *U.S. News and World Report*, 28 July 1986, p. 48.
12. President's Commission, p. 27.

13. Ibid., p. 16.
14. Boffey, p. A1.
15. "Cause of Bissell's Death Ruled A Drug Overdose," *The New York Times*, 18 February 1988, p. C21.
16. Richard Within, "Cocaine Traces are Found in Pilot Who Died in Crash," *The New York Times*, 12 March 1988, p. 7.
17. Donna Boundy, "Cocaine Accounts for Much in Steinberg Case," *The New York Times* (Letters to the Editor), p. 26.
18. Peter Kerr, "New Violence Seen in Users of Cocaine," *The New York Times*, 7 March, 1987, p. 29.
19. President's Commission, p. 24.
20. Jacob V. Lamar, "Where the War is Being Lost," *Time*, 14 March 1988, pp. 21–22.
21. Ibid.
22. Peter Kerr, "Cocaine Study Finds Recent Use in Most Arrested," *The New York Times*, 22 January 1988, p. A1.
23. National Commission on Marijuana and Drug Abuse, *Drug Abuse in America: Problem in Perspective* (Washington: Government Printing Office, 1973), p. 81.
24. "Engineer in Amtrak Crash Guilty of Manslaughter in Plea Bargain," *The New York Times*, 17 February 1988, p. A10.
25. President's Commission, p. 60.
26. Ibid., p. 65.
27. Alvin E. Bessent, "Copiague Man on Trial in Fatal Arson," *Newsday*, 31 March 1988, p. 23.

CHAPTER 3

1. Richard H. Blum and Associates, *The Dream Sellers* (San Francisco: Jossey-Bass, Inc., 1972), p. 210.
2. Ibid., p. 203.
3. Jeffrey Fagan, Bruce Johnson, and Steven Belenko, *Crack and Changing Patterns of Drug Use, Abuse, and Criminality* (New York: Criminal Justice Agency, 25 February 1987), p. 4.
4. Blum, p. 205.
5. Allen J. Beck, "Survey of Youth in Custody, 1987," (Washington, D.C.: U.S. Department of Justice, Bureau of Justice Statistics) September 1988.
6. Blum, p. 107.
7. Jacob V. Lamar, "Kids Who Sell Crack," *Time*, 14 March 1988, pp. 21–22.
8. Ibid.

9. Blum, p. 163.
10. Lamar, p. 22.
11. Lamar, p. 22.
12. James A. Inciardi, *The War on Drugs* (Palo Alto, Calif.: Mayfield, 1986), p. 164.
13. Ibid., p. 164.
14. Josh Barbanel, "Crack Use Pervades Life in a Shelter," *The New York Times*, 18 February 1988, pp. A1, B3.
15. "Thieves Stab Boy and Get $1,000," *The New York Times*, 14 February 1988, p. B5.
16. Esther Iverem, "A Teen-Age Addict Is Held in the Killings of 5 in East Harlem," *The New York Times*, 10 January 1988, pp. 1, 26.

CHAPTER 4

1. Peter Blayner, " 'Fat Cat' and the Crack Wars: Brash Young Dealers Murder the Drug Establishment," *New York*, 7 September 1987, pp. 46–54.
2. Peter Kerr, "30 Arrested in Drug Sweep in Queens," *The New York Times*, 12 August 1988, pp. B1, B2.
3. Selwyn Raab, "Brutal Drug Gangs Wage War of Terror in Upper Manhattan," *The New York Times*, 15 March 1988, p. B1.
4. Tom Morganthau, "The Drug Gangs," *Newsweek*, 28 March 1988, pp. 20–27.
5. Ibid.
6. Leonard Buder, "Federal-City Efforts Attack Violent Brooklyn Drug Ring," *The New York Times*, 11 March 1988, p. B3.
7. Morganthau, p. 25.
8. Robert Reinhold, "In the Middle of L.A.'s Gang Warfare," *The New York Times Magazine*, 22 May 1988, pp. 30–74.
9. Morganthau, p. 26.
10. Reinhold, p. 30.
11. William Robbins, "Armed, Sophisticated, and Violent, Two Drug Gangs Blanket the Nation," *The New York Times*, 25 November 1988, p. A1.
12. Morganthau, p. 26.
13. James N. Baker, "Crack Wars in D.C.," *Newsweek*, 22 February 1988, pp. 24, 25.
14. Isabel Wilkerson, "Detroit Drug Empire Showed All the Traits of Big Business," *The New York Times*, 18 December 1988, p. 1.
15. Raab, p. B1.
16. Reinhold, p. 30.
17. Ibid.

18. A. M. Rosenthal, "The Murder of Rosa Urena," *The New York Times*, 20 May 1988, p. A31.
19. "870 Arrested in Effort to Halt Gang Violence," *The New York Times*, 19 September 1988, p. A15.

CHAPTER 5

1. President's Commission on Organized Crime, *America's Habit, Drug Abuse, Drug Trafficking and Organized Crime* (Washington, D.C.: Government Printing Office, 1986), p. 5.
2. Pico Iyer, "Fighting the Cocaine Wars," *Time*, 25 Feb. 1985, p. 26.
3. Paul Eddy, *The Cocaine Wars* (New York: W. W. Norton and Co., 1988), p. 47.
4. Mary H. Cooper, "The Business of Illicit Drugs," *Editorial Research Reports*, (Washington, D.C.: Congressional Quarterly, Inc.), 20 May 1988, p. 22.
5. Jack Anderson, "Drug Cartel's Next Targets," *Newsday*, 19 September 1988, p. 62.
6. Jon Nordheimer, "In A Quiet Setting U.S. Concludes Biggest Drug Trafficking Case," *The New York Times*, 11 May 1988, p. A23.
7. Ibid.
8. Anderson, p. 62.
9. Ibid.
10. Nordheimer, p. A23.
11. Anderson, p. 62.
12. Peter Kerr, "Cocaine Glut Pulls New York Market Into Drug Rings' Tug-of-War," *The New York Times*, 24 August 1988, pp. B1, B5.
13. President's Commission, p. 16.
14. Ibid., p. 23.
15. Peter Kerr, "Chinese Crime Groups Rising to Prominence in New York," *The New York Times*, 4 January 1988, pp. A1, B4.
16. Brian Freemantle, *The Fix: Inside the World Drug Trade* (New York: Tom Doherty Associates, 1986), p. 147.
17. Michael Satchell, "Reign of an Opium Warlord," *U.S. News and World Report*, 4 May 1987, p. 33.
18. Cooper, p. 22.
19. Freemantle, p. 19.
20. Ibid., p. 170.
21. Ibid., p. 168.
22. Ibid., p. 270.
23. Ibid., p. 271.
24. Ibid., p. 316.
25. Ibid., p. 317.

CHAPTER 6

1. Peter Kerr, "12,000 Form Ranks to Mourn Two Slain Policemen," *The New York Times*, 23 October 1988, pp. 1, 36.
2. Tom Morganthau, "The Drug Gangs," *Newsweek*, 28 March 1988, pp. 20–27.
3. Ibid.
4. Howard Abadinsky, *Organized Crime* (Boston: Allyn and Bacon, Inc., 1981), p. 166.
5. James N. Baker, "Crack Wars in D.C.," *Newsweek*, 22 February 1988, pp. 24, 25.
6. Peter Kerr, "Firepower Rises in Federal Drive on Drug Sellers," *The New York Times*, 8 April 1988, pp. A1, B5.
7. Baker, p. 25.
8. Ronald S. Lauder, *Fighting Violent Crime in America* (New York: Dodd, Mead, 1988), p. 31.
9. George Volsky, "Two Former Policemen in Miami Are Found Guilty of Drug Charges," *The New York Times*, 10 February 1988, p. A29.
10. Georgette Bennett, *Crime Warps: The Future of Crime in America* (Garden City, N.Y.: Doubleday, 1987), p. 218.
11. Abadinsky, p. 172.
12. Paul Eddy, *The Cocaine Wars* (New York: W. W. Norton and Co., 1988), p. 20.
13. NIDA, *Drugs and Crime: The Relation of Drug Use and Concommitant Criminal Behavior* (Washington: Government Printing Office, 1976), p. 61.
14. Bennett, p. 148.
15. Peter Kerr, "Citizen Anti-Crack Patrols: Vigilance or Vigilantism?" *The New York Times*, 23 May 1988, pp. B1, B4.
16. Jenny Abdo, "Muslim Law on LI Street Corner," *Newsday*, 15 February 1988, p. 3.
17. Mark Moore, *Drug Trafficking* (Washington: National Institute of Justice, 1988), p. 3.

CHAPTER 7

1. E. R. Shipp, "The Perilous Right of Citizens to Make Their Own Arrests," *The New York Times*, 19 June 1988, Sec. 4, p. 8.
2. Elaine Scolino with Stephen Engelberg, "Fighting Narcotics: US Is Urged to Shift Tactics," *The New York Times*, 10 April 1988, pp. 1, 10.

3. Elaine Scolino, "Ambitious Eradication Goals and Withering Obstacles," *The New York Times*, 10 April 1984, p. 10.
4. Eileen Shannon, *Desperados: Latin Drug Lords, US Lawmen and the War America Can't Win* (New York: Viking, 1988), p. 100.
5. Scolino, "Fighting Narcotics," p. 10.
6. Ibid., p. 10.
7. President's Commission on Organized Crime, *America's Habit, Drug Abuse, Drug Trafficking, and Organized Crime* (Washington: Government Printing Office, 1986), p. 169.
8. Scolino, "Fighting Narcotics," p. 10.
9. Mark Miller, "The Southwest Drug Connection," *Newsweek*, 23 November 1987, p. 30.
10. Mark Moore, *Drug Trafficking* (Washington: National Institute of Justice, 1988), p. 4.
11. Scolino, "Fighting Narcotics," p. 10.

BIBLIOGRAPHY

Newspapers and weekly newsmagazines are prime sources of information on the subject of violence and drugs. Nearly all issues include reports of studies or developments, or articles on some aspect of the issue.

PUBLICATIONS

Annals of the American Academy of Political and Social Science. *The Police and Violence,* November 1980.

Bureau of International Narcotics Matters. *International Narcotics Control Strategy Report,* 1 March 1988.

Comptroller General of the United States. "Controlling Drug Abuse: A Status Report," 1988.

Department of State Bulletin. "Links Between International Narcotics Trafficking and Terrorism," August 1985.

Editorial Research Reports. "The Business of Illicit Drugs," 20 May 1988.

John Jay College of Criminal Justice. "Contributions of Delinquency and Substance Use to School Dropout," September 1988.

Journal of Drug Issues. "The Drugs/Violence Nexus: A Tripartite Conceptual Framework," Fall 1985.

Narcotic and Drug Research. "Homicide Related to Drug Traffic." June 1986.

National Institute of Justice. "Drug Trafficking," 1988.

———. "Probing the Links Between Drugs and Crime," February 1985.

———. "Controlling Drug Abuse and Crime," March/April 1987.

———. "State Prison Inmate Survey, 1986: Drug Use and Crime," July 1988.

———. "Violent Crime Trends," November 1987.

———. "Federal Offenses and Offenders: Drug Law Violators, 1980–1986," June 1988.

———."Drugs and Violence," December 1969.

National Institute on Drug Abuse. *Drugs and Crime: The Relation of Drug Use and Concomitant Criminal Behavior,* 1976.

National Narcotics Intelligence Consumers Committee (NNICC). "The NNICC Report 1987: The Supply of Illicit Drugs to the U.S.," April 1988.

New York City Criminal Justice Agency. "Crack and Changing Patterns of Drug Use/Abuse and Criminality," 25 February 1987.

President's Commission on Organized Crime. *America's Habit: Drug Abuse, Drug Trafficking, and Organized Crime: Report to the President and the Attorney General,* 1986.

BOOKS

Abadinsky, Howard. *Organized Crime.* Boston: Allyn and Bacon, Inc., 1981.

Bennett, Georgette. *Crimewarps: The Future of Crime in America.* Garden City: Doubleday, 1987.

Blum, Richard H., and associates. *The Dream Sellers.* San Francisco: Jossey-Bass, Inc., 1972.

Dolan, Edward F. *International Drug Traffic.* New York: Franklin Watts, 1985.

Eddy, Paul. *The Cocaine Wars.* New York: W. W. Norton and Co., 1988.

Freemantle, Brian. *The Fix: Inside the World Drug Trade.* New York: Tom Doherty Associates, 1986.

Grainspon, Lester. *Cocaine: A Drug and Its Social Evolution.* New York: Basic Books, 1985.

Hawkes, Nigel. *The Heroin Trail.* New York: Gloucester Press, 1986.

Inciardi, James A. *The War on Drugs.* Palo Alto: Mayfield Publishing Co., 1986.

Kaplan, John. *The Hardest Drug: Heroin and Public Policy.* Chicago: University of Chicago Press, 1983.

Kramer, Rita. *At A Tender Age: Violent Youth and Juvenile Justice.* New York: Holt and Co., 1988.

Lauder, Ronald S. *Fighting Violent Crime in America.* New York: Dodd, Mead, 1985.

Mille, James. *The Underground Empire.* New York: Doubleday, 1986.

Moore, Mark H. *Buy and Bust: The Effective Reduction of an Illicit Market in Heroin.* Lexington, MA: D.C. Heath, 1977.

Musto, David. *The American Disease: Origins of Narcotics Control.* New York: Oxford University Press, 1987.

V., Rachel *Family Secrets, Life Stories of Adult Children of Alcoholics.* New York: Harper and Row, 1987.

Rock, Paul E. *Drugs and Politics.* New Brunswick, NJ: Transaction Books, 1977.

Shannon, Eileen. *Desperados, Latin Drug Lords, U.S. Lawmen, and the War America Can't Win.* New York: Viking, 1988.

Traub, James. *The Billion Dollar Connection: The International Drug Trade.* New York: Julian Messner, 1982.

Trebach, Arnold S. *The Great Drug War.* New York: Macmillan Publishing Co., 1987.

INDEX

Adams, Harold E., 26
Addiction, 22, 25, 27, 28
Addicts, 10, 16, 45
Adolescence, 36. *See also* Juveniles
Afghanistan, 92–93
Aggravated assault, 12
AIDS, 24, 43, 89
Alcohol abuse, 20–21
Amphetamines, 13–14, 16
    legal use of, 89, 90
    trafficking of, 71–73
Anderson, Jack, 64
Angel dust. *See* PCP
Antidrug activism, 83–84
Armstrong, Robert, 53
Arson, 12
Aryan Brothers, 73
Assault, 12
Automobile accidents, 21

Bandidos, 72
Barbiturates, 16, 89, 90
Battery, 12
Belushi, John, 25

Bissell, Patrick, 25
Black Guerrilla, 73
Black Tar, 22, 67
Bloods, 52
Blum, Richard H., 34, 35, 38, 40
Bolivia, 91
Bonilla, Rodrigo, 65
Bruno organized-crime family, 73
Buy-and-bust operations, 97
Byrne, Edward, 49, 57

Cali cartel, 65–66
Cannabis sativa. *See* Marijuana
Chambers brothers, 54–56
Child abuse, 10
China White, 22, 31
Chinese Connection, 68–69
Citizen patrols, 83–84
Cocaine, 14, 16–17, 24–25
    eradication of crops, 90, 93
    growth and processing of, 62–63
    heroin used with, 25
    legalization of, 88–90
    suicide among users, 23–24

Cocaine (*continued*)
    trafficking, 61–66, 90
    See also Crack
Cocaine psychosis, 26
Colombian drug traffickers, 61–66, 70, 74, 93
La Cosa Nostra, 61, 67, 68
Crack, 13–14, 16–17, 26–28
    danger to children of, 41
    street-corner cartels, 47, 48
    See also Cocaine
Crack gangs, 50. *See also* Drug gangs
Crime. *See also* Violent crime; Drug gangs
    drug use and, 10–14, 32
    organized, 60–61, 71–74. *See also* Drug trafficking
    public response to, 16–17, 83–84
    street, 43–44, 47–49
Crime rate, 17–18, 40
Crips, 52, 53
Cuartas, Belisario Betancur, 64

Decoy, 79
Delinquency, 36. *See also* Juveniles
Depressants, 71, 89, 90
Designer drugs, 30–32, 71–74
    See also LSD, PCP
Diazepam (Valium), 71
Drive-by murder, 52
Drug abuse. *See also* Addiction
    efforts to curb, 17
    relationship of crime to, 10–15, 32
Drug abusers:
    entry into drug culture of, 16
    frequency of crime among, 11
    juvenile, 15, 18, 34–36, 38
    police as, 80–81
Drug culture, 15–16
Drug dealing. *See also* Drug trafficking

Drug dealing (*continued*)
    gang warfare and, 49–56
    hustling and, 37–39
    preparation for, 34–37
    prostitution and, 41–43
    street crime and, 43–44
    street-corner cartels and, 47–49
    witness reprisals and, 56–57, 77
    violence and, 39–41, 54–56
Drug Enforcement Administration (DEA), 69, 72, 78
Drug gangs, 49–56, 71–73
Drug kingpins, 47, 76–77, 85, 96–97
Drug trafficking. *See also* Drug dealing
    attempts to destroy, 90–98
    cocaine, 61–66
    Colombian, 61–66, 70
    heroin, 66–69
    marijuana, 70–71
    Mexican, 67, 68, 70
    and terrorists, 93
Drugs, illegal:
    cost of, 14
    effects of, 32
    eradication of crops producing, 90–94
    legalization of, 88–90
    major, 10, 11
    trends in use of, 16–18

Ecstasy, 31
Edwards, Delroy, 51
Employment, 14
Eradication of illicit crops, 90–94

Family structure, 37, 45, 50
Fetal alcohol syndrome, 21
Firearms, 39, 40, 78
Free-basing, 24
French Connection, 67

Gangs. *See* Drug gangs
Gaviria, Escobar, 65

Godbolt, Thomas (Mustaffa), 49
Gold, Mark, 25, 26
Golden Crescent, 69
Golden Triangle, 68, 69
Goldstein, Paul J., 12
Gonnabees, 52
Grant, John, 21
Guinses, V. G., 53
Gunberg, Jeffrey, 27
Guns, 39, 40, 78

Hallucinogens, 30–32, 71
    See also LSD
Hashish, 28. See also Marijuana
Hayes, Richard, 84
Hell's Angels, 72
Heroin, 15, 16, 22–23
    eradication of crops of, 90
    growth and processing, 66
    legalization of, 88–90
    trafficking of, 66–69, 90
    U.S. income from sale of, 66
    used with cocaine, 25
    user profiles, 22–23
Herrera organization, 67–68
Herrington, Lois Haight, 18
Homicide, 12
    committed by teenagers, 18
    drug use and, 13
    gang warfare and, 54
    of innocent bystanders, 57–
        58, 78
    intimidating effect of, 80
    of witnesses, 56–57
Hoyos, Carlos Mauro, 65
Hoyt, William K., Jr., 56
Hustling, 37–39
Hypodermic needles, 24

Inciardi, James A., 42, 43
Informants, 77–78
Inhalants, 16
Interdiction, 95–96

Jackson, Edward, 73
Jamaican gangs, 50–51
Johnson, Sterling, 76

Jumpout, 79
Juveniles:
    alcohol use by, 20–21
    in drug gangs, 50, 54–55, 59
    drug taking by, 18, 34–36,
        38
    entry-level positions in drug
        trade for, 34–41
    as part of drug culture, 15
    prostitution among, 41–43
    violence and, 10, 34–42

Kirkpatrick, Jane, 21
Kirkwood, Richard, 31–32
Koch, Edward, 76

Lara Bonilla, Rodrigo, 64
Law-enforcement efforts, 96–98
    See also Police
Lawn, John C., 65
Lookout, 35
Los Angeles gangs, 51–53
LSD, 16, 30, 73. See also Designer
    drugs; Hallucinogens

MacDonald, Donald Ian, 26–27
Mafia families, 74
Maoist Shining Path, 93
Marijuana, 16, 17, 28–29
    eradication of crops of, 90–
        91, 93
    growth and processing, 70
    interdiction of, 96
    research uses of, 89
    trafficking of, 70–71, 90
Medellín cartel, 63–66
Mental illness, 27
Messing up, 35
Methadone, 11, 22
Mexican drug trafficking, 67, 68,
    70
Mexican Mafia, 73
Miami Boys, 54
Mob yuppies, 74
Motorcycle gangs, 71–74
Moyer, Thomas, 51
Muslim patrols, 83–84

Musto, David F., 17

Narcotics Task Force, 79
National Commission on Marijuana and Drug Abuse, 28
Neighborhood citizen patrols, 83–84
Nichols, Lorenzo (Fat Cat), 47–49
Nixon, Richard M., 16
Noriega, Manuel Antonio, 64, 92
Nuestra Familia, 73

Off-loading, 70
O.G. (old gangsters), 53
Opium, 66
Organized crime, 60–61, 71–74
"Outlaws," 72
Overdose, 22, 25

Pagans, 72–73
Panama, 92
Paraquat, 70
PCP, 13–14, 16, 30–32. *See also* Designer drugs
Police:
    drug-related crime and, 76–80, 85–86
    lack of confidence in, 83
    use of violence by, 80–82
Posses, 50, 51
Pregnancy:
    AIDS and, 24
    alcohol use and, 21
    crack use and, 27
Prisons, 17, 73, 81
Prostitution, 41–43

Racketeer Influenced and Corrupt Organizations Act (RICO), 79
Railroad workers, 29
Rape, 12, 20
Reppetto, Thomas A., 81
Robbery, 13
Runner, 36

Sa, Khun, 69
Schlesinger, Steven R., 11
Sets, 52
Sicilian Mafia, 61
Speedball, 25
Steinberg, Joel B., 26
Stimulants. *See* Amphetamines
Street crime, 43–44. *See also* Crime; Violent crime
Street-corner cartels, 47–49
Stutman, Robert M., 66
Suicide, 23–24
Survey of Inmates of State Correctional Facilities (Justice Department), 11
Synthetic drugs. *See* Designer drugs

Taylor, Carl, 54, 55
Terrorists, 93
Tranquilizers, 71, 89, 90
Trebach, Arnold S., 18
Triad, 68
Turner, Maurice, Jr., 54, 78

Untouchables, 53–54

Valium (diazepam), 71
Vigilantism, 83–84
Violent crime, 12–16, 43–44
    alcohol use and, 20–21
    cocaine and, 25–26
    crack and, 26–28
    hallucinogens and, 31–32
    heroin use and, 23–24
    dealing and, 39–43, 47–59
    marijuana and, 29
    police and, 78
    prostitution and, 42–43
    trafficking and, 61–74
    See also Crime

Wannabees, 52
Witnesses, 56–57, 77
Works, 24